Dynamic Business Strategy

MW01034053

Inspiring the Next Game: Strategy Ideas for Forward Looking Leaders

BCG Henderson Institute

Dynamic Business Strategy

—

Competing in a Fast-changing, Uncertain Context

Edited by
Martin Reeves and François Candelon

DE GRUYTER

ISBN 978-3-11-075527-5
e-ISBN (PDF) 978-3-11-075538-1
e-ISBN (EPUB) 978-3-11-075550-3
ISSN 2701-8857

Library of Congress Control Number: 2021946581

Bibliographic information published by the Deutsche Nationalbibliothek
The Deutsche Nationalbibliothek lists this publication in the Deutsche Nationalbibliografie;
detailed bibliographic data are available on the internet at http://dnb.dnb.de.

© 2022 The BCG Henderson Institute
Cover image: sesame/DigitalVision Vectors/Getty Images
Typesetting: Integra Software Services Pvt. Ltd.
Printing and Binding: LSC Communications, United States

www.degruyter.com

Acknowledgments

We would like to acknowledge all of the authors whose work appears in this collection: Lewis Baker, Michael Deimler, Jack Fuller, TejPavan Gandhok, Kaelin Goulet, James Yuji Grosvenor, Peter Hamilton, Ryoji Kimura, Julien Legrand, Rich Lesser, Hen Lotan, Claire Love, Sandy Moose, Yves Morieux, Saumeet Nanda, Ron Nicol, Frida Polli, Martin Reeves, Filippo Scognamiglio, George Stalk, Hiroaki Sugita, Thijs Venema, and Kevin Whitaker.

We would also like to acknowledge the broader BCG Henderson Institute community: our Fellows, Ambassadors, and operations teams over the years, who have all made invaluable contributions to our research; our academic collaborators, who have expanded our horizons of new ideas; and our BCG practice area partners, who have collaborated with us on several of these articles.

https://doi.org/10.1515/9783110755381-202

About the BCG Henderson Institute

The BCG Henderson Institute is the Boston Consulting Group's think tank, dedicated to exploring and developing valuable new insights from business, technology, economics, and science by embracing the powerful technology of ideas. The Institute engages leaders in provocative discussion and experimentation to expand the boundaries of business theory and practice, and to translate innovative ideas from within and beyond business.

https://doi.org/10.1515/9783110755381-203

Contents

Acknowledgments —— V

About the BCG Henderson Institute —— VII

Introduction —— XI

Part I: Updating the Classical Strategy Playbook

Martin Reeves, Michael Deimler, George Stalk,
and Filippo Scognamiglio
Chapter 1
Revisiting the Rule of Three and Four —— 3

Martin Reeves, George Stalk, and Filippo Scognamiglio
Chapter 2
Revisiting the Experience Curve —— 9

Rich Lesser, Martin Reeves, and Kaelin Goulet
Chapter 3
Revisiting Time-Based Competition —— 15

Martin Reeves, Sandy Moose, and Thijs Venema
Chapter 4
Revisiting the Growth-Share Matrix —— 19

Part II: Mastering New Strategic Capabilities

Martin Reeves, Michael Deimler, Yves Morieux, and Ron Nicol
Chapter 5
Adaptive Advantage —— 29

Martin Reeves, Peter Hamilton, and Kevin Whitaker
Chapter 6
The Elusive Quest for Adaptability —— 35

Martin Reeves, Thijs Venema, and Claire Love
Chapter 7
Shaping to Win —— 39

Martin Reeves, Julien Legrand, and Jack Fuller
Chapter 8
Your Strategy Process Needs a Strategy —— 45

Martin Reeves, Frida Polli, TejPavan Gandhok, Lewis Baker, Hen Lotan,
and Julien Legrand
Chapter 9
Your Capabilities Need a Strategy: Choosing and Developing the Right
Ones for Each Environment —— 57

Part III: **Expanding the Boundaries of Strategy**

Ryoji Kimura, Martin Reeves, and Kevin Whitaker
Chapter 10
The New Logic of Competition —— 71

Martin Reeves, Ryoji Kimura, Hiroaki Sugita, Saumeet Nanda, and James
Yuji Grosvenor
Chapter 11
The Challenge of Slow —— 81

BCG Henderson Institute
Chapter 12
Strategy on Multiple Timescales —— 93

Martin Reeves, Kevin Whitaker, and Saumeet Nanda
Chapter 13
Fractal Strategy: Responding to COVID-19 Effectively on Multiple
Timescales —— 109

List of Figures —— 119

Index —— 121

Introduction

The playing field for business has changed significantly in recent decades. Technological progress is accelerating, causing any particular offering or business model to become obsolete or commoditized more quickly. As a result, competition has become more dynamic: outperformers are losing their advantage more quickly, on average, and business lifespans are shrinking.

The business context has also become less certain. Economic and political uncertainty has risen dramatically and is likely to remain at elevated levels, driven in part by inequality and social polarization. Competitive uncertainty has also risen – whereas companies historically competed in well-defined industries against a stable set of peers, technology is blurring the boundaries of industries, increasing the potential paths to competitive disruption.

As a result of these developments, some have asked whether strategy has become less important.[1] In fact, strategy is not dead – the differential performance between winners and losers across industries is actually increasing over time. However, the playbook for strategy needs to be reinvented for today's business environment.

Traditionally, strategy has focused on static sources of competitive advantage. These include economies of scale and learning, positioning of a company's portfolio of businesses, and differentiation of their products. These advantages have not gone away, but in a faster-changing environment their role has been diminished. They have been complemented by new dimensions of competition, such as adapting to unpredictable contexts, shaping malleable ones, and surviving harsh conditions (including economic downturns or periods of industry disruption).

The scope of strategy must be expanded and evolved accordingly. Traditionally, leaders have considered a narrow range of timescales in setting their strategy – in many cases, fixed cycles such as a one-year financial plan and a five-year strategic plan. Such efforts have generally focused only on the business and its immediate competitors and customers, taking the broader external context as given. Strategy today needs to consider a much greater range of timescales – from the rapid speed of AI algorithms (which operate on scales of milliseconds) to the slow-moving pace of larger issues such as climate change (which play out over decades or longer) that are now becoming more relevant and impactful. It must also consider the broader social, political, and environmental context, which can have significant implications for businesses if not addressed.

---

1 See, for instance, Rita G. McGrath, *The End of Competitive Advantage*, Harvard Business Review Press, 2013.

https://doi.org/10.1515/9783110755381-205

This book discusses the new role of strategy in a dynamic, unpredictable context, drawing on the work of the BCG Henderson Institute and its fellows and ambassadors over several years. Part I, "Updating the Classical Strategy Playbook," revisits some canonical strategy frameworks and whether or not they are still relevant – showing that while they are still useful, they need to be updated for the modern era. Chapter 1 revisits the rule of three and four, finding that the classic rules for market dynamics have held up in many industries but not some dynamic and unstable ones. Chapter 2 revisits the experience curve, arguing that companies need to accumulate an additional kind of experience to sustain competitive advantage. Chapter 3 revisits the concept of time-based competition, showing how companies today need to not only act faster but also learn faster and more effectively. And Chapter 4 revisits the growth-share matrix, Bruce Henderson's famous framework for portfolio strategy, and the enhancements needed to apply it today.

Part II, "Mastering New Strategic Capabilities," discusses the new strategic capabilities companies need today, such as adapting to uncertain environments and shaping new or disrupted ones. Chapter 5 introduces "adaptive advantage," the ability to evolve the organization to outcompete peers in turbulent environments. Chapter 6 lists myths that can get in the way of creating adaptive businesses. Chapter 7 discusses "shaping" strategies and how they can help companies gain advantage in emerging or shifting markets. Chapter 8 lays out different strategy processes that are best-suited for different contexts, and Chapter 9 identifies the resulting strategy skills needed to thrive in them.

Part III, "Expanding the Boundaries of Strategy," examines broadening the outer limits of strategy. Chapter 10 outlines a new logic of competition – new capabilities, such as learning, imagination, and resilience, that are necessary to create dynamic advantage. Chapter 11 describes the new challenge of slow-moving forces, such as demographic change, that are increasingly relevant for businesses. Chapter 12 discusses multi-timescale strategy broadly, informed by perspectives from a wide range of fields across business, sustainability, and science. Chapter 13 closes by illustrating how the challenge of managing on multiple timescales applied throughout the COVID-19 crisis.

We hope that this volume will help business professionals as well as academics and students with an interest in strategy understand the new competitive challenges that businesses face and develop a playbook to address them.

Part I: **Updating the Classical Strategy Playbook**

Martin Reeves, Michael Deimler, George Stalk,
and Filippo Scognamiglio

Chapter 1
Revisiting the Rule of Three and Four

In "The Rule of Three and Four," written in 1976, Bruce Henderson put forth an intriguing hypothesis about the evolution of industry structure and leadership. He posited that a "stable, competitive" industry will never have more than three significant competitors. Moreover, that industry structure will find equilibrium when the market shares of the three companies reach a ratio of approximately 4:2:1.

Henderson noted that his observation had yet to be validated by rigorous analysis. But it did seem to map closely with the then-current structures of a wide range of industries, from automobiles to soft drinks. He believed that even if the hypothesis were only approximately true, it would have significant implications for businesses.

Fast-forward to the modern day. Has the rule of three and four held? If so, to what degree? Does it merit the attention of today's decision makers? Our analysis yielded compelling findings.

Testing the Rule of Three and Four

To test Henderson's theory, the BCG Strategy Institute (the predecessor of the BCG Henderson Institute), working in collaboration with academics from Chapman, Claremont, and Rutgers universities, studied industry data from more than 10,000 companies dating back to 1975.[1] This analysis allowed us to confirm that Henderson's hypothesis was indeed valid when he conceived it: it accurately described the market share structures current at the time, and trends in a wide range of industries. We can also confirm that the rule of three and four has remained a predictor of the evolution of industry structures in "stable, competitive" industries over the decades, with the caveat that many industries have experienced a departure from such stable conditions.

---

1 Our research, performed in collaboration with Professors Can Uslay, Ekaterina Karniouchina, and Ayça Altintig, employed Standard Industrial Classification (SIC) designations. Data were sourced from S&P Compustat's database. In total, we studied more than 10,000 companies, from nearly 450 industries, representing more than $18 trillion in revenue in 2009.

https://doi.org/10.1515/9783110755381-001

To facilitate our analysis, we divided companies into two categories: those with market shares of more than 10 percent ("generalists") and those with shares of 10 percent or less. The prevalence of industries with no more than three generalists (the "three" part of Henderson's rule) was striking. From 1976 through 2009, industries with one, two, or three generalists ranged from 72 percent to 85 percent and averaged 78 percent. The most common industry structure throughout the period was the three-generalist configuration, which prevailed in 13 of those 34 years and was the second-most common in 20 out of 34 years.

Industries with three-generalist structures have also proven the most profitable for industry participants, with an average return on assets a full 2.5 percentage points higher than in industries with four, five, or six generalists. Additionally, three- and two-generalist configurations appear to have the greatest stability and to act as the strongest "basins of attraction" – that is, more companies gravitate toward these structures every year than toward any other (Figure 1.1).

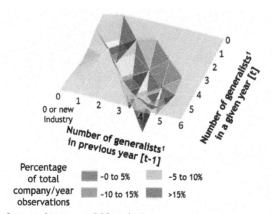

Source: Compustat; BCG analysis
Note: N=121,859 company/year observations, >10,000 companies, and approximately 450 industries from 1975 to 2009. Industries were aggregated based on four-digit SIC codes
1. Companies or segments of companies with a revenue market share equal to or greater than 10 percent of overall industry revenues in any given year

Figure 1.1: Three- and two-generalist configurations appear to have the greatest stability and to act as the strongest "basins of attraction".

Our study also confirmed the "four" part of Henderson's rule – the 4:2:1 market-share ratio that tends to characterize equilibrium in these industries. Over the period studied, the top players in nearly 60 percent of industries with three-generalist structures had relative market shares of 1.5x to 2.5x, quite close to Henderson's prediction of 2.0x. And we confirmed that today, the 4:2:1 relationship is the most prevalent among industries led by three generalists.

Current examples of the rule of three and four are easy to find. The U.S. rental-car industry is one (Figure 1.2). In 2006, four competitors – Avis, Enterprise Holdings, Hertz, and Vanguard Car Rental – had market shares exceeding 10 percent. The March 2007 acquisition of Vanguard by Enterprise, however, gave the latter nearly half the market – and set in motion competitive dynamics implicit in the rule of three and four. In fact, the market has closely followed Henderson's script. In 2011, the three market leaders – Enterprise, Hertz, and Avis – had market shares of 48 percent, 22 percent, and 14 percent, respectively, close to the 4:2:1 ratio Henderson predicted. Hertz's 2012 acquisition of Dollar Thrifty, which held a 3 percent market share at the time, made the numbers align even more closely with the rule.

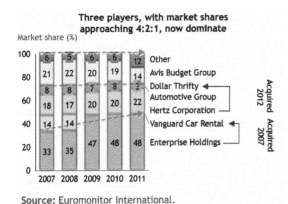

Figure 1.2: The evolution of the U.S. rental car industry illustrates the rule of three and four.

All told, the rule of three and four appears to be very much alive and well today. But its applicability, as Henderson proposed, remains confined to "stable, competitive" industries characterized by low turbulence and limited regulatory intervention. Other examples of industries where the rule applies today include machinery manufacturing (companies such as John Deere, Agco, and CNH), household appliances (Whirlpool, Electrolux, and GE), and credit-rating agencies (Experian, Transunion, and Equifax).

The rule of three and four does not seem to apply to the growing number of more dynamic, unstable industries, such as consumer electronics, investment banking, life insurance, and IT software and services. Nor does it apply to industries where regulation hinders genuine competition or industry consolidation, such as telecommunications in the U.S. (for example, the U.S. government's antitrust action against the merger of AT&T and T-Mobile).

The difference in applicability is stark. For companies in low-volatility industries led by three generalists, we measured a return on assets 6.1 percentage points higher than that of companies in low-volatility industries led by a larger number of generalists. Yet we found no such trend in high-volatility industries – the three-generalist configuration had no advantage over others. A possible explanation for this is that experience curve effects, which Henderson supposed underpinned the rule, are less applicable in industries where technological innovation and other factors shift the basis of advantage before the benefits of a lower cost position can be realized.

Rising turbulence in many industries has also reduced the rule's impact over time. The higher return on assets associated with three-generalist structures, for example, has decreased, falling from an average of approximately 3 percentage points in the 1970s to roughly 1 percentage point today. The same holds true for the prevalence of the 4:2:1 market-share ratio among industries led by three generalists – that ratio is still the most common in such industries, but it is less common than it was at its peak.

Implications for Decision Makers

For corporate decision-makers, the rule of three and four has important implications. First, an understanding of the industry environment is critical. Is the industry one in which classical "rules" of strategy, such as the rule of three and four, apply? Or does it demand an alternative – for example, an adaptive – approach?[2] Next, decision makers must determine whether their company has a long-term viable position in its industry. Where the rule applies, this is largely determined by market share. Being an industry's largest player is the most desirable position; and the number two and three spots are also sustainable. Any other position is likely to be unsustainable.

Once they understand their company's position, decision makers must shape their strategies accordingly. If the company is a top-three player, it should aggressively defend its share. If it is outside the top three, it should attempt to improve its position through consolidation or by shifting the basis of competition – or it should exit the industry. (As Henderson wrote, ". . . cash out as soon as practical. Take your writeoff. Take your tax loss. Take your cash value. Reinvest in products and markets where you can be a successful leader.") If the company operates in an

---

2 See "Your Strategy Needs a Strategy," *Harvard Business Review*, September 2012.

environment where the rule does not apply, it should employ adaptive or shaping strategies, which we will describe elsewhere.[3]

The rule has implications for other stakeholders as well. Investors, for example, should factor an industry's dynamics and likely trajectory into their investment strategies. And policy makers should consider the rule and its ramifications as they weigh antitrust issues.

As we have seen, the rule of three and four remains relevant more than three decades after its conception – in a business environment that is, in many respects, profoundly different – and its implications continue to provide guidance for decision makers working in environments where classical business strategies hold. For companies in increasingly unstable environments, a new set of rules applies, calling for more adaptive approaches to strategy.

---

3 See "Adaptability: The New Competitive Advantage," *Harvard Business Review*, July 2011.

Martin Reeves, George Stalk, and Filippo Scognamiglio
Chapter 2
Revisiting the Experience Curve

The *experience curve* is one of BCG's signature concepts and arguably one of its best known. The theory, which had its genesis in a cost analysis that BCG performed for a major semiconductor manufacturer in 1966, held that a company's unit production costs would fall by a predictable amount – typically 20 to 30 percent in real terms – for each doubling of "experience," or accumulated production volume. The implications of this relationship for business, argued Bruce Henderson, were significant.[1] In particular, he said, it suggested that market share leadership could confer a decisive competitive edge, because a company with dominant share could more rapidly accumulate valuable experience and thus achieve a self-perpetuating cost advantage over its rivals.

The experience curve theory proved a valuable descriptor and predictor of competitive dynamics across much of the business landscape through the 1970s, providing a sound guide for investment and pricing decisions and an invaluable tool for strategists. Is the idea applicable to today's environment? Yes, but in some industries it is no longer sufficient by itself as a blueprint for competitive advantage. In contrast to the 1960s and 1970s, when the general business environment was relatively stable and new-product introduction relatively infrequent, today's business climate is characterized by higher volatility, less stable industry structures, and frequent product launches in response to rapidly changing technologies and tastes.

Experience of the type addressed by the experience curve is still necessary – often critically so, depending on the industry. But we argue that most companies today need an additional kind of experience if they hope to create and sustain competitive advantage.

Two Types of Experience

The type of experience that the classic experience curve refers to – the ability to produce existing products more cheaply and deliver them to an ever-wider

---

1 See "The Experience Curve," BCG Perspectives, 1968; and "The Experience Curve – Reviewed (Part I)," BCG Perspectives, 1974.

https://doi.org/10.1515/9783110755381-002

audience – can be considered experience in *fulfilling* demand. This type of experience remains very important in many industries, especially those that are relatively stable, cost-sensitive, competitive, and production-intensive.

Hard-disk drives, for example, showed a cost decline of about 50 percent for each doubling of accumulated production from 1980 through 2002, bringing the average cost per gigabyte from $80,000 in 1984 to $6 in 2001. Laser diodes showed a similarly steep cost decline of 40–45 percent with each doubling of volume, with prices decreasing from the roughly $30,000 of fiber amplifiers in the early 1980s to $1.30 for 0.8-micrometer CD lasers (unpackaged) in 1999. But to win in today's environment, many companies also need experience in *shaping* demand, or creating demand for new products and services.

Figure 2.1 is a visual representation of the two types. Experience in fulfilling demand is represented as the classic experience curve: it shows a reduction in costs as a function of cumulative volume (which is a straight line in a log-log scale). Experience in shaping demand is represented as repeated "jumps" across successive experience curves, representing a company's ability to move from product generation to product generation repeatedly and successfully. The relationship between the two types of experience might also be visualized as an endless version of the popular board game *Chutes and Ladders*. To maintain competitive advantage, companies have to both "slide down snakes" (that is, fulfill demand) and "climb ladders" (that is, shape demand). The relative emphasis on each depends on a company's particular circumstances.

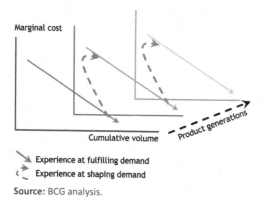

Experience at fulfilling demand
Experience at shaping demand

Source: BCG analysis.

Figure 2.1: The relationship between experience in *fulfilling* demand and experience in *shaping* demand.

The two types of experience are inherently different, as is the way they are accumulated and the benefits they confer. Experience at fulfilling demand is acquired through a logical deductive process: capture your cost data, analyze them, determine opportunities for improvement, implement changes, iterate. The main features of the learning process are repetition and incremental improvement, both explicit and implicit. Experience at shaping demand, in contrast, is acquired through an inductive process: sample consumer behaviors, formulate a hypothesis on unmet needs or imagine the possibilities permitted by new technologies, test the hypothesis with a new offering, shut down the test or expand it based on empirical results, formulate new hypotheses based on the latest empirical results, repeat.

It should be noted that neither experience type, by itself, has ever been sufficient for long-term competitive advantage. Both have always been necessary. What has changed recently is that the requisite speed of cycling between the two has increased dramatically. We refer to this ability to develop and leverage both existing and new product knowledge concurrently, or to switch between them effectively over time, as *ambidexterity*.[2]

Experience in Shaping Demand in Practice

Experience in shaping demand – which can be gauged by a company's product-introduction "clock speed" or by the percentage of sales derived from new products or services – can be a powerful competitive weapon, particularly when paired effectively with experience in fulfilling demand. It can be seen as a second-order type of experience, one that comes from sharing experience across different areas and learning how to learn new things. It includes the ability to "forget" lessons from the past when such information has become obsolete and is no longer relevant to the latest product generation. This type of experience can be disruptive not only because it involves innovation but also because being at a disadvantage on an earlier product generation can quickly be overturned by shaping demand and getting a head start on the next experience curve.

We illustrate the power of demand-shaping experience, and how the past and present of the experience curve interweave, by taking a contemporary look at the industry that gave birth to the experience curve.

ARM Holdings is a leading semiconductor player, with particular strength in the design of low-power microprocessors. The company itself is not a

---

[2] "Ambidexterity: The Art of Thriving in Complex Environments," *BCG Perspectives*, February 2013.

manufacturer; rather, it designs the underlying technologies and leaves manufacturing to its partners. By focusing on shaping demand through its innovative designs and leveraging its partners' expertise in fulfilling demand, thus avoiding the need to develop such experience itself, ARM has created a compelling recipe for success. Devices based on ARM's technology accounted for 95 percent of the fast-growing smartphone market as of 2012. ARM also boasted an impressive annualized total shareholder return (TSR) of 28 percent for the seven years through 2011. ARM's partners, too, have benefited from this approach, as evidenced by their strong product shipments and TSR: Qualcomm's annualized TSR for the same period was 5 percent, for example, also above the industry median of –6 percent for the same period.[3]

Facebook successfully shaped demand for its services by continually improving users' experience and doing so faster than rival MySpace (Figure 2.2). To build demand-shaping experience, Facebook released new software weekly and experimented with new technologies and features such as live chat, photo albums, and a third-party app-developer interface. These efforts allowed Facebook to gain a more thorough understanding of users' needs and desires and respond to them with accelerated new-product generation, and translating into a swelling userbase and eventually an improved cost position.

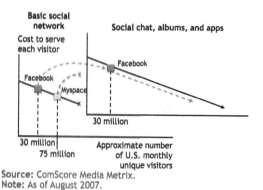

Source: ComScore Media Metrix.
Note: As of August 2007.

Figure 2.2: Facebook shaped demand for its services faster than rival MySpace.

Netflix twice radically shaped demand by improving the convenience of a service. Its promise of convenient and inexpensive DVDs by mail (with no late fees

---

3 This industry median is based on a comparable-period analysis of the TSR of 174 North American companies identified by the Standard Industrial Classification code 3674 for semiconductors and related devices.

or hassles with pickup and drop-off) successfully shaped the demand for home video. Netflix succeeded again when it introduced streaming (which added the benefits of assured and instant availability), even though the offering was obviously going to cannibalize the company's DVD-by-mail business. Netflix realized that the DVD-by-mail offering was vulnerable to streaming technology, regardless of which company launched the service first. The company's early move to shape demand forced its major competitors to react to the initial consumer expectations that Netflix had set, giving Netflix a substantial advantage.

These companies' focus on excellence in both shaping and fulfilling demand allowed them to thrive, often overtaking their established competitors. This is a phenomenon that the traditional experience curve cannot explain.

Sustaining Competitive Advantage Both within and Across Product Generations

Solidifying long-term competitive advantage in today's environment requires asking a series of questions about excellence in both shaping and fulfilling demand.

- *What balance of experience in fulfilling and shaping demand is required in our industry?* In some industries, experience in fulfilling demand remains critical.[4] Other industries, usually younger ones, will benefit more from experience in shaping demand. Determine what your industry requires. Remember that, as illustrated by ARM Holdings, experience can be sourced externally under certain circumstances.
- *Do we have the right disciplines and capabilities to develop and leverage experience in fulfilling demand?* Build scale and defend the market share of your established products. Learn through repetition and incremental improvement, both explicit and implicit, to further reduce costs.
- *Do we have the right disciplines and capabilities to develop and leverage experience in shaping demand?* Unlink the development of new products and services from the production and management of existing ones. Empower individuals to experiment. Foster an appetite for risk with incentives that reward success; punish failure only if it arises from irresponsibility. Accelerate

---

4 See, for example, "Investigating the Impact of Experience Curves on the Development of Brazil's Presalt Cluster: Applying Experience Curves to Oil-Field Development," BCG article, September 2011.

the product life cycle and plan the retirement of products as well as their launch. Create advantage by better understanding and shaping demand.

- *Do we have the right metrics in place for both types of experience?* Ensure that you can gauge your prowess in building and leveraging both types of experience. Compare the results with those of your direct and indirect competitors. Examine your relative cost positions and demand-shaping clock speed and use them as your firm's composite measure of success.

- *Do we have the right approach to balancing and combining experience types?* Shaping demand and fulfilling demand are different in nature, and experience is acquired and leveraged through different, sometimes conflicting, means. In our above-referenced *BCG Perspectives* publication on ambidexterity, we presented four different approaches to striking an optimal balance: separation, switching, self-organizing, and external ecosystem. The right approach for your company will be determined by the dynamism and diversity of your specific industry environment.

As consumer tastes and product generations change ever more rapidly, experience in fulfilling demand alone is no longer sufficient to sustain a competitively advantaged position. An additional type of experience – experience in shaping demand – becomes necessary as well. This experience must be acquired through new and different means that can sometimes be in direct conflict with the current means your organization employs to acquire experience. But failure to do so can exact a significant toll, ranging from the loss of a leadership position to outright business failure.

The ability to skillfully build and leverage both types of experiences concurrently – *ambidexterity* – is the present-day hallmark of truly exceptional management. It is a rare attribute but a highly valuable one, one that can be developed if a company follows the right approach.

Rich Lesser, Martin Reeves, and Kaelin Goulet

Chapter 3
Revisiting Time-Based Competition

Nearly 25 years after the book's publication in 1990, Apple CEO Tim Cook was known to give his colleagues copies of *Competing Against Time: How Time-Based Competition Is Reshaping Global Markets*, the seminal work by BCG's George Stalk and Tom Hout. Why does the leader of one of the world's most innovative companies consider it a still-worthwhile read?

Traditionally, businesses strove to produce high-quality goods at the lowest possible cost. But Stalk and Hout taught the business world that the added element of speed was ultimately the key to competitive advantage. Stalk had observed Japanese companies that were not scale leaders in their industries reaping advantage by shortening their product-development cycles and factory-process times – essentially managing time the way that most businesses managed costs, quality, and inventory. This "flexible manufacturing" approach also reduced variety-related costs at the companies. Consequently, despite their smaller size and volumes, these companies could produce fewer goods but with greater diversity and quality than their competitors – and do so at lower cost (Figure 3.1).

Automobile suspension components		
	U.S. Competitor	Japanese Competitor
Annual volume (millions of units)	10	3.5
Number of employees		
direct	107	50
indirect	135	7
Total	242	57
Annual units per employee	41,300	61,400
Types of finished parts	11	38
Unit cost for comparable part (index)	**$100**	**$49**

Source: George Stalk, Jr., "Time: The Next Source of Competitive Advantage," *Harvard Business Review*, July-August 1988.

Figure 3.1: Companies using time-based competition could produce fewer goods but with greater diversity and quality than their competitors at lower cost.

https://doi.org/10.1515/9783110755381-003

The acceleration of cycle times not only allowed companies to remove waste from the process, it also provided a host of competitive benefits. By responding more quickly, companies enhanced their productivity and also gained favor with customers, thereby achieving higher market share. By embracing the principles of time-based competition (TBC), these businesses also reduced complexity and rework and increased transparency, allowing them to break the assumed tradeoff between cost and quality.

TBC's impact on business thinking ultimately proved enormous, with companies across sectors embracing it and its popular derivative, process reengineering, to streamline and accelerate their operations. Sun Microsystems (acquired by Oracle in 2010) achieved market dominance by halving the time required to design and introduce engineering workstations. Honda gained ground by introducing 113 new models in the time it took its close competitor Yamaha to create 37. Jack Welch announced that GE's core principles would be "speed, simplicity, and self-confidence."

Zoom forward to today, when the pace of change seems faster than ever: technologies are evolving increasingly quickly, economic power is shifting to emerging markets, and many business models are becoming obsolete. As a result, an unprecedented number of long-standing incumbent companies seem to be questioning how they do business.

Companies are attempting to meet the demands of this time-compressed reality in both new and traditional ways. They are exploiting 3D printing, for example, to reduce the time it takes to produce prototypes; deploying automated factories to shrink change-over times; enabling greater customization and closer proximity to customers; and leveraging big data and analytics to make it easier to identify and act on opportunities.

Common to all of these efforts is the recognition of the growing primacy of speed. Words like "agility" are increasingly on the lips of CEOs. Said Jeremy Stoppelman, CEO of Yelp, "You have to be very nimble and very open-minded. Your success is going to be very dependent on how you adapt." It's a view that extends well beyond the big-tech arena. As Mitchell Modell, CEO of Modell's Sporting Goods, observed, "The big never eat the small – the fast eat the slow."

So, are we headed back to the future? Is Tim Cook right? Is it time to dust off the BCG classic and re-reengineer our core processes? The answer to all three questions is yes – but with several important qualifiers.

Without a doubt, the pace of change is now faster than ever. Many businesses have evolved into essentially information businesses, and many more are critically dependent upon increasingly complex signals and information.

Companies now, therefore, need to act at the "speed of data." This is a tough quantitative challenge, requiring new technologies and techniques to bridge gaps between the intrinsic speed and flexibility of data on one hand, and people, organizations, and physical assets on the other. It is also a qualitative challenge, requiring many companies to rethink their business models.

UPS, a package delivery firm, may not seem like a digital company. But living up to its "Moving at the Speed of Business" tagline requires sophisticated and dynamic integration, analysis, and aggressive data management. UPS's front-line employees use data to meet performance objectives. Truck drivers, for example, use route-optimization algorithms to decide whether to save a mile of driving or to deliver a package 15 minutes early. To avoid overwhelming employees, the company refines the display of information; to make workers more comfortable with on-the-job analytics, it utilizes familiar platforms, such as smartphones. UPS also prioritizes continuous improvement to become faster still: it is building real-time, adaptive analytics into the next version of its logistics software, for instance.

Whereas TBC was about doing a predictable set of activities faster, companies now also need to be able to learn how to do new things faster and more effectively. Agility is insufficient – companies now also need to be adaptive. In today's era of accelerated change, new products, technologies, and business models can arise before companies have had a chance to fully optimize existing ones. Figure 3.2 shows how telephone technology illustrates this phenomenon at work.

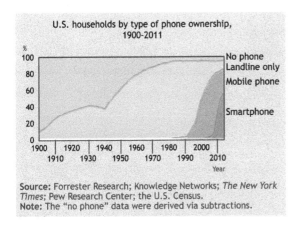

Figure 3.2: U.S. households by type of phone ownership 1900–2011.

Alibaba, China's dominant retailer, exemplifies "TBC 2.0" and its virtuous cycle of data, speed, learning, innovation, and growth. Every day, Alibaba's three server centers process more than a petabyte of data – the equivalent of three times the storage space needed for all the DNA information of the U.S. population. With that data firepower, Alibaba is driving an economic transformation in Chinese retailing – delivering more products faster and to more people via more, new, and different business models.

And with speed and data come learning and business model innovation. Via AliPay, Alibaba's customers can now pay for online purchases and invest their savings, and businesses can obtain loans. Companies and governments can store data on Alibaba's cloud-computing services; and other retailers, such as Haier and Nike, can set up online store fronts through Tmall.com, Alibaba's business-to-consumer platform. Alibaba is using speed, information, and innovation to tap the burgeoning power of Chinese consumption by creating a single, truly nationwide market.

Today's need not only for speed but also for adaptiveness should spur managers to shift their mindset about the imperatives necessary to survive and succeed in a TBC 2.0 world. For an increasing number of businesses, these imperatives include the following:

– Reconceiving your business as an information business
– Ensuring that your organization can respond at the speed of data
– Recognizing that the basis for competitive advantage has shifted from scale, position, and speed to adaptiveness
– Cultivating and measuring rapid learning
– Balancing the exploitation of existing opportunities and business models with the exploration of new ones
– Breaking free from yesterday's successful business model

Time-based competition is more relevant than ever. Companies must now not only run faster but also adapt to keep up.

Martin Reeves, Sandy Moose, and Thijs Venema
Chapter 4
Revisiting the Growth-Share Matrix

*We are managing our businesses with a laser-like focus on return on capital . . . rigorously
testing our portfolio to identify which businesses to grow, run for cash, fix or sell.*
— The Dow Chemical Company, Annual Report 2012

Decades after Bruce Henderson proposed BCG's *growth-share matrix*, the concept is very much alive. Companies continue to need a method to manage their
portfolio of products, R&D investments, and business units in a disciplined and
systematic way. *Harvard Business Review* named it one of the frameworks that
changed the world. The matrix is central in business school teaching on strategy.

At the same time, the world has changed in ways that have a fundamental
impact on the original intent of the matrix: Since 1970, when it was introduced,
conglomerates have become less prevalent, change has accelerated, and competitive advantage has become less durable. Given all of that, is the BCG growth-
share matrix still relevant? Yes, but with some important enhancements.

The Original Matrix

*A company should have a portfolio of products with different growth rates and different mar-
ket shares. The portfolio composition is a function of the balance between cash flows . . .
Margins and cash generated are a function of market share.*
— Bruce Henderson, "The Product Portfolio," 1970

At the height of its success, in the late 1970s and early 1980s, the growth-share
matrix (or approaches based on it) was used by about half of all Fortune 500
companies, according to estimates.[1]

The matrix helped companies decide which markets and business units to
invest in on the basis of two factors – company competitiveness and market at-
tractiveness – with the underlying drivers for these factors being relative market
share and growth rate, respectively. The logic was that market leadership, expressed through high relative share, resulted in sustainably superior returns. In

---

1 Philippe C. Haspeslagh, "Portfolio Planning: Uses and Limits," *Harvard Business Review*,
January 1982. https://hbr.org/1982/01/uses-and-limits.

https://doi.org/10.1515/9783110755381-004

the long run, the market leader obtained a self-reinforcing cost advantage through scale and experience[2] that competitors found difficult to replicate. High growth rates signaled the markets in which leadership could be most easily built.

Putting these drivers in a matrix revealed four quadrants, each with a specific strategic imperative. Low-growth, high-share "cash cows" should be milked for cash to reinvest in high-growth, high-share "stars" with high future potential. High-growth, low-share "question marks" should be invested in or discarded, depending on their chances of becoming stars. Low-share, low-growth "pets" are essentially worthless and should be liquidated, divested, or repositioned given that their current positioning is unlikely to ever generate cash.

The utility of the matrix in practice was twofold:

1. The matrix provided conglomerates and diversified industrial companies with a logic to redeploy cash from cash cows to business units with higher growth potential. This came at a time when units often kept and reinvested their own cash – which in some cases had the effect of continuously decreasing returns on investment. Conglomerates that allocated cash smartly gained an advantage.
2. It provided companies with a simple but powerful tool for maximizing the competitiveness, value, and sustainability of their business by allowing them to strike the right balance between the exploitation of mature businesses and the exploration of new businesses to secure future growth.

The BCG Matrix in a Changing World

The world has changed. Conglomerates have become far less prevalent since their heyday in the 1970s. More importantly, the business environment has changed.

First, companies face circumstances that change more rapidly and unpredictably than ever before because of technological advances and other factors. As a result, companies need to constantly renew their advantage, increasing the speed at which they shift resources among products and business units. Second, market share is no longer a direct predictor of sustained performance (Figure 4.1). In addition to market share, we now see new drivers of competitive advantage, such as the ability to adapt to changing circumstances or to shape them.

So what do these two shifts mean for the original portfolio concept? We might expect that these developments translate into changes in the distribution of businesses across the matrix. As change accelerates, we may see that businesses move

---

2 https://www.bcg.com/publications/1968/business-unit-strategy-growth-experience-curve.

Increased speed of changes ...

Time between innovation and adoption[1]

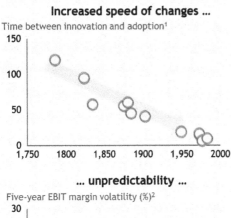

... unpredictability ...

Five-year EBIT margin volatility (%)[2]

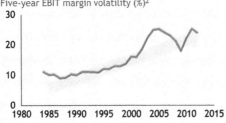

... reduced importance of market share

Probability that share leader is also profit leader[3]

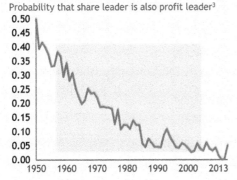

Source: BCG analysis.
[1]Time in years.
[2]Average five-year standard deviation of EBIT margin.
[3]Sales versus operating margin.

Figure 4.1: Market share is no longer a direct predictor of sustained performance.

around the matrix quadrants more quickly. Similarly, as the disruption of mature businesses increases with change and unpredictability, we may see proportionately lower numbers of cash cows because their longevity is likely in many cases to be curtailed.

To test these hypotheses, we looked closely at the effect of these changes in the U.S. economy, by treating individual companies as analogs for individual business units in a conglomerate's portfolio. In our analysis, we assigned every publicly listed U.S. company to a portfolio quadrant, on the basis of its growth rate and market share.[3]

The results robustly support the hypotheses.

First, companies indeed circulated through the matrix quadrants faster in the five-year period from 2008 through 2012 than in the five-year period from 1988 through 1992. This was true in 75 percent of industries, reflecting the higher rate of change in business overall. In those industries, the average time spent in a quadrant halved: from four years in 1992 to less than two years in 2012. To further test this hypothesis, we also studied ten of the largest U.S. conglomerates and discovered that the average time any business unit spent in a quadrant was less than two years in 2012.[4] Only a few, relatively stable industries, such as food retail and health-care equipment, saw fewer disruptions and hence did not show faster circulation.

Second, our analysis showed the breakdown of the relationship between relative market share and sustained competitiveness. Cash generation is less tied to mature businesses with high market share: In our analysis of public companies, the share of total profits captured by cash cows in 2012 was 25 percent lower than it was in 1982 (Figure 4.2). At the same time, the duration of that later part of the life cycle declined as well, on average by 55 percent in those industries that witnessed faster matrix circulation.

---

3 The analysis was based on all publicly listed U.S. companies from 1980 through 2012 as provided by Compustat. Relative growth rate is the difference between the company growth rate and the market growth rate, with high being above market average and low being below market average. Relative market share is a company's market share divided by the market share of the industry's third-ranked company in terms of share. Companies were segmented by Global Industry Classification Standard to determine appropriate market segments and market growth rates. The average time spent in a quadrant was calculated for the five-year periods from 1988 through 1992 and from 2008 through 2012.

4 We studied the following companies: Carlisle Companies, Danaher, Disney, The Dow Chemical Company, DuPont, General Electric, Loews, Procter & Gamble, 3M, and Textron.

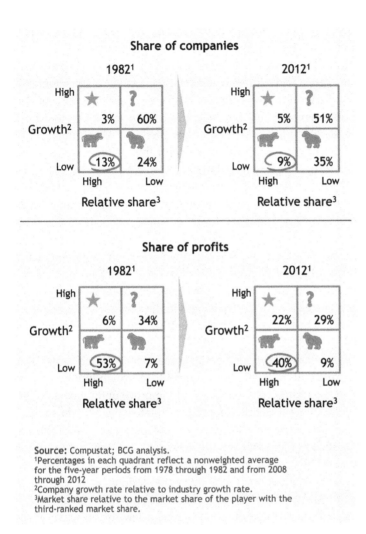

Figure 4.2: The breakdown of the relationship between relative market share and sustained competitiveness.

The Continued Relevance of the BCG Matrix

We keep speed in mind with each new product we release. . . . And we continue to work on making it all go even faster. . . . We're always looking for new places where we can make a difference.

– Google's company-philosophy statement

Given the rapid pace and unpredictable nature of change in today's market-place, the question arises: Has the growth-share matrix lost its value?

No, on the contrary – however, its significance has changed. It needs to be applied with greater speed and with more of a focus on strategic experimentation to allow adaptation to an increasingly unpredictable business environment. The matrix also requires a new measure of competitiveness to replace its horizontal axis now that market share is no longer a strong predictor of performance. Finally, the matrix needs to be embedded more deeply into organization behavior to facilitate its use for strategic experimentation.

Successful companies today need to explore new products, markets, and business models more frequently to continuously renew their advantage through disciplined experimentation. They also need to do so more systematically to avoid wasting resources, a function the matrix has successfully fulfilled for decades. This new experimental approach requires companies to invest in more question marks, experiment with them in a quicker and more economical way than competitors, and systematically select promising ones to grow into stars. At the same time, companies need to be prepared to respond to changes in the marketplace, cashing out stars and retiring cows more quickly and maximizing the information value of pets.

Google is a prime example of such an experimental approach to portfolio management, as expressed in its mission statement: "Through innovation and iteration, we aim to take things that work well and improve upon them in unexpected ways." Its portfolio is a balanced mixture of relatively mature businesses such as AdWords and AdSense, rapidly growing products such as Android, and more nascent ones such as Glass and the driverless car.

But at Google, portfolio management is not just a high-level analytical exercise. It is embedded in organizational capabilities that facilitate strategic experimentation. Google's well-known exploratory culture ensures that a large number of ideas get generated. From these question marks, a few are selected on the basis of rigorous and deep analytics. Subsequently, they are tried out on a restricted basis, before being scaled up.

Gmail and Glass, for instance, were launched among a select group of enthusiasts. Such early testing not only keeps costs per question mark down but also helps the company reduce the risk of new-product launches. After launch, Google leverages deep analytics to continuously monitor portfolio health and move products around the matrix. As a result, it is able to launch and divest approximately 10 to 15 projects every year.

BCG Matrix 2.0 in Practice

To get the most out of the matrix for successful experimentation in the modern business environment, companies need to focus on four practical imperatives:

1. Accelerate. It is critical to evaluate the portfolio frequently. Businesses should increase their strategic clock-speed to match that of the environment, with shorter planning cycles and feedback loops requiring simplified approval processes for investment and divestment decisions.

2. Balance exploration and exploitation. This requires having an adequate number of question marks while simultaneously maximizing the benefits of both cows and pets:
- *Increase the number of question marks.* This requires a culture that encourages risk taking, tolerates failure, and allows challenges to the status quo.
- *Test question marks quickly and economically.* Successful experimenters achieve this by using rapid (for example, virtual) tests that limit the cost of failure.
- *Milk cows efficiently.* Successful companies do not neglect the need to exploit existing sources of advantage. They milk low-growth businesses by improving profitability through incremental innovation and streamlining of operations.
- *Keep pets on a short leash.* With experimentation comes failure: our analysis found that the number of pets increased by almost 50 percent in 30 years. Although Bruce Henderson asserted that pets were worthless, today's successful companies capture failure signals from pets to inform future decisions on where and how to experiment. Additionally, they attempt to lower exit barriers and move quickly to squeeze out remaining value before divestment.

3. Select rigorously. Companies must carefully select investments as well as divestments. Successful companies leverage a wide range of data sources and develop predictive analytics to determine which question marks should be scaled up through increased investment and which pets and cows to divest proactively.

4. Measure and manage portfolio economics of experimentation. Understanding the experimentation level required to maintain growth is important for long-term sustainability:
- *Manage the rate of experimentation.* Successful companies continually measure and manage the number and costs of the question marks they generate to ensure their pipeline stays filled.
- *Drive new product and business success.* Companies need to ensure that the probability that question marks become stars is high enough – and that the

cost of failure for these question marks is acceptable – in order to sustain growth from new products.
- *Maintain a portfolio balance.* Successful companies look for today's stars (and question marks) to ultimately generate at least enough profitability to replace cows (and pets) that are later in their life cycle so that the company portfolio generates sufficient profitability in the long run.

Increasing change certainly requires companies to adjust how they apply the matrix. But it does not undercut the power of the original concept. What Bruce Henderson wrote years ago still holds today, perhaps even more so than ever: "The need for a portfolio of businesses becomes obvious. Every company needs products in which to invest cash. Every company needs products that generate cash. And every product should eventually be a cash generator; otherwise it is worthless. Only a diversified company with a balanced portfolio can use its strengths to truly capitalize on its growth opportunities."

Part II: **Mastering New Strategic Capabilities**

Martin Reeves, Michael Deimler, Yves Morieux, and Ron Nicol

Chapter 5
Adaptive Advantage

Increased turbulence in the business environment has invalidated an implicit and critical assumption of classical business strategy: that competition is sufficiently stable and predictable for the basis of competitive advantage to be readily determined. Traditional approaches to strategic planning become futile in a world in which the key variables are constantly shifting and difficult to forecast.

We can distinguish three important dimensions of turbulence: (1) volatility in market positions, (2) unpredictability of outcomes, and (3) the widening gap in performance between winners and losers. Most industries have experienced instability on at least one of these dimensions, but some – such as technology-driven industries and commercial banking – have been affected on all three. The hardest-hit industries are those that have been disproportionately affected by globalization, deregulation, digitalization, connectivity, deconstruction, and the shift from products to services. Most companies, and especially those in industries characterized by both unpredictability and a high rate of change, need a more adaptive and dynamic approach to strategy – an approach that emphasizes iterative experimentation in order to overcome the limitations of deductive approaches and keep pace with incessant change.

With such an approach, organizations gain adaptive advantage: the ability to achieve superior outcomes in a turbulent environment by continuously reshaping the enterprise through a process of managed evolution. In this chapter, we explain how adaptive advantage can be harnessed in practice.

Elements of Adaptive Advantage

Three attributes are essential for survival in a changing environment: (1) readiness, (2) responsiveness, and (3) resilience. They can be achieved by static measures such as improved forecasting, decentralized decision-making, and buffering with excess capacity, respectively. However, to gain a sustainable advantage in a turbulent environment, companies must employ a fourth, more dynamic, *recursive* approach to determine which better-fitting strategies continuously evolve in response to change (Figure 5.1).

Recursion occurs through a four-component iterative process comprising variation, selection, and amplification, with modulation at its center (VSAM).

https://doi.org/10.1515/9783110755381-005

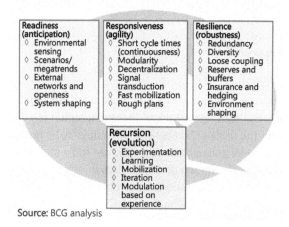

Source: BCG analysis

Figure 5.1: Essential attributes for survival in a changing business environment.

1. *Variation.* Novelty is essential in responding to a changing environment. Methods of achieving variation include targeted innovation and natural or induced modification of internal practices. Responding to signals from the external environment or leveraging the innovative capacities of external stakeholders can also be used to generate variation.
2. *Selection.* Variation alone will not allow companies to adapt to a changing environment. The most promising variations must be selected through such mechanisms as stage gates and portfolio management, pilot projects or limited tests, and full-scale tests conducted directly in the marketplace.
3. *Amplification.* Selected variations must be scaled up, optimized, and, where appropriate, hard-wired into the routines and structures of the organization, either through a formal and deliberate process of resource allocation or indirectly, through internal or external competition.
4. *Modulation.* Modulation is the locus of strategic intent. It shapes and fine-tunes the other three components of the adaptive system in response to the environmental context and corporate goals and capabilities. Adaptive strategy is thus quite different from biological evolution, in which no overarching will or intention is at work.

Although each component in the VSAM loop may seem familiar, the adaptive approach is unlike classical strategy in a number of fundamental respects. First, it works by modulating the context from which new strategies emerge, rather than specifying exactly what those new strategies should be. Second, it largely erases the distinction between planning and implementation, since successful strategies emerge from practice rather than from analysis and design. The discipline of adaptive strategy therefore centers on the choices a company makes in the VSAM loop in order to fit the adaptive mechanism to the environmental context.

Styles of Adaptive Strategy

There are many ways of executing and modulating the activities of the VSAM loop. The choices relate principally to four factors:

1. *Degree of proactivity.* Do the adaptive mechanisms anticipate and shape change, or do they simply react effectively to it?
2. *Degree of modification.* Is adaptation directed merely at the level of products and processes or, more fundamentally, at the level of the business model or the extended business system?
3. *Degree of exploration.* Is the focus on refining and exploiting a successful model, or on exploring new frontiers and possibilities?
4. *Degree of intentionality.* Are the adaptive mechanisms primarily analytical, structured, programmed, and deliberate, or do they emerge indirectly as a result of either internal or external collaboration or competition?

A company's optimal choices are mainly a function of the environment – especially the rate at which it is changing, the predictability of change, and the degree of change required. There are four broad styles of adaptive strategy (Figure 5.2).

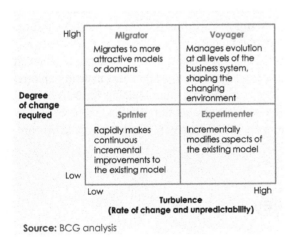

Source: BCG analysis

Figure 5.2: The four styles of adaptive strategy.

1. *The Sprinter.* In environments with only a moderate degree of both turbulence and required change, companies can focus on rapidly optimizing and exploiting existing business models to track an increasingly volatile environment. The fashion retailer Zara, for example, focuses on building a fast feedback cycle between sales data from its stores and the design and manufacture of new products. This model allows the company to stay at the forefront of fashion trends without having to make big bets on where the trends are headed.

2. *The Experimenter.* In environments where turbulence is high but the degree of change required is low, companies whose business models are fundamentally sound must nevertheless modify their product mix or other low-level aspects of their business through a process of iterative experimentation. McDonald's, for example, uses a structured process to design, test, and introduce menu items while keeping its overarching business model unchanged. This enables it to evolve along with customer preferences and still preserve the well-honed efficiency of the kitchen model at the core of its operations.

3. *The Migrator.* In environments with moderate turbulence and a high degree of required change, companies must deliberately migrate their obsolescent business models or domains toward more attractive ones using a targeted and deliberate process. Virgin, for instance, systematically manages a diverse portfolio of challenger businesses by rapidly scaling up potential winners and cleanly divesting or shutting down losers.

4. *The Voyager.* In environments with a high degree of both turbulence and required change, companies need to deploy an exploratory approach to the business model or system. This can involve "live" tests with a mixed portfolio of competing business models and strategies, some of which may even be mutually contradictory. Netflix, which has reinvented fundamental aspects of its business strategy and model several times in the extremely turbulent movie-rental business, is a good example of a voyager. It removed late fees (at one time a mainstay of industry profits) and instead explored video streaming on a variety of platforms, cannibalizing its DVD-by-mail business in order to stay ahead of the competition. Netflix has succeeded in dominating and reshaping a chaotic industry in which less adaptive competitors have fared poorly.

Beginning the Journey

Adaptive advantage is a powerful concept for companies facing unstable environments. It involves not just different ways of *operating* but also very different ways of *thinking* about strategy. The first step in embracing adaptive advantage is therefore to create awareness of the challenges and opportunities presented by turbulence and unpredictability – and the adaptive choices available.

Leaders can begin the journey by asking their management teams to consider five basic questions:

1. How rapidly and fundamentally is the basis of advantage changing in our industry?
2. How effectively are we tracking, shaping, and adapting to these changes?
3. What is the cost of not adapting to change?
4. Which of the four styles of adaptive strategy – sprinter, experimenter, migrator, or voyager – would be most appropriate, given our environment and situation?
5. What practices, capabilities, or beliefs are creating bottlenecks in our ability to embrace and deploy adaptive advantage?

We believe that adaptive advantage will increasingly supplement the traditional advantages of position and capability, and prove important for survival in a changing business environment.

Martin Reeves, Peter Hamilton, and Kevin Whitaker
Chapter 6
The Elusive Quest for Adaptability

Business leaders have often espoused adaptability – the ability to change in concert with changing circumstances. With technology continuing to drive business model disruption, with political and economic uncertainty at elevated levels even before the COVID-19 crisis, and with outperformance regressing to the mean faster,[1] what could be more timely?

We know a lot about how to adapt. From planned experimentation, through digital A-B testing, mind stretching scenarios and zero-based budgeting, to always-on strategy and new organizational models, many tomes have been written and read on the topic.

Yet companies and institutions seem to have a hard time walking the talk. The late Clay Christensen's work reminds us that many fail to heed the imperative to self disrupt before being disrupted, in spite of evidence that clearly shows pre-emption is the best option. And for all the fascination with alternative ways of organizing to better match the current business environment, nearly all companies still organize based on Max Weber's original principles of bureaucracy, which are predicated on stability rather than change.

What is so hard about adaptation? Ten false beliefs can get in the way of the mental, behavioral, and structural changes necessary for adaptation.

Myths of What Adaptation is:
1. *"Adaptation is optimization."* Adaptation is evolution. In a very loose sense, organisms adapt by continuously optimizing for their changing environment by creating new variants, seeing what works, and amplifying successes. Business optimization is mostly pursued in the exact opposite fashion, however. Companies reduce costs and increase profitability by reducing variance, which is the lifeblood of evolutionary learning. 100% efficiency means no variance, which means no learning new things. Optimizing is *not* adapting.
2. *"Adaptation is merely a slogan."* Management ideas turn over often, and companies incorporate them into their vocabularies very rapidly. Recently

1 https://sloanreview.mit.edu/article/fighting-the-gravity-of-average-performance/.

https://doi.org/10.1515/9783110755381-006

we have seen an explosion in the use of words like "adaptation," "agile," "lean," and "ecosystem." There is a tendency for such new ideas to be used in a broad but shallow manner, such that everything seems to be an example of the idea in question, but strict definition becomes elusive. Then the value of the idea is lost. This is also true of adaptation. The tragedy is that adaptation is not only a fashionable piece of jargon, but also the precise idea that evolutionary change needs to be embraced by business organizations.

3. *"Adaptation is not businesslike."* The large organizations with which we are familiar were born in more stable times, times that permitted and required planning, strict roles, and disciplined implementation. As a result, many large organizations have acquired a culture where clear intentions, constancy of plans, consistency of practice and discipline in execution have become prized virtues. Measured against this, inconsistency, change, trial-and-error, and serendipity can seem to be somehow unsubstantial and less worthy. Such implicit biases undermine the messy but effective process of adaptation.

Myths of What Adaptation Requires:

4. *"Failure is bad."* We have all heard that fast, repeated failure is the route to effective learning. But organizations often directly and indirectly reward behavioral models that imply the exact opposite. It's not that failure is good in itself, but that adaptation involves trying new things, some of which don't work out. Failure is therefore a necessary by-product of adaptation. A few years ago in a conversation with former Chairman of the Joint Chiefs of Staff, General Martin Dempsey, General Dempsey reflected that, at the time, one of his biggest challenges was that the upper ranks of the military were populated with people who had never failed, whereas combatting problems like the rapid evolution of improvised explosive devices required tremendous adaptability and therefore the experience of failure.

5. *"We can't just throw spaghetti at the wall."* Actually, we can – and to some extent we must – if we want our organizations to adapt. More precisely, we need to act in unplanned ways and embrace the serendipity of things working unexpectedly well in order to adapt effectively. That is, we need to create variance and embrace emergent strategies. Of course, we don't have to throw all of the spaghetti at all of the walls – experimentation is likely to be more valuable in fast evolving, emerging businesses. Experiments should also be granular enough to not risk the entire business with any one trial and can be guided by hypotheses.

6. *"Business needs to be grounded in the here and now."* Certainly, adaptation to changing circumstances should be guided by experimentation and

observation. But larger leaps have to first be imagined. The mind has a key role to play in innovation. Indeed, one of our unique human attitudes, which is beyond the reach of current AI, is the ability to think counterfactually. Machine learning, for all its transformative potential, does not replace this need for creativity. We can test hypotheses more efficiently, but the hypotheses must come from somewhere. Imagining possibilities increases our sensitivity to accidents and anomalies that lead in the desired direction. We should remember that stressing "practicality" is as arbitrary as stressing "imagination" – and both are required to sustain a business.

7. *"Without alignment, there would be chaos."* Adaptation alternates between divergence (creating variation) and convergence (selection and amplification). Embracing variance is perfectly consistent with selection and alignment around a continuous stream of better, new approaches. Maximal alignment around yesterday's successful ideas is not an effective path to learning new ways of doing things.

Myths of What Roles are Played in Adaptation:

8. *"Executives plan and decide."* In stable times, executives review market analyses, review past competitive positioning and performance, and create enduring plans. In today's digital environment, however, competitors and disruptors are constantly testing new moves. Hierarchies cannot match the clock speed of digital innovation. Counterintuitive as it sounds, action must now sometimes precede analysis.

9. *"Managers and workers execute."* Again, in stable times, the plan is created on high in the executive team or strategy function (albeit with inputs from the front line) and the job of the rest of the organization is to execute it in a disciplined fashion. Adaptation, in contrast, comes from the front line trying different approaches in different situations, learning what works and sharing that knowledge, which is then embraced by the rest of the organization through codification and amplification. This requires the empowerment to try new things and a culture of "act first, apologize later."

10. *"Adaptation is something that organizations do."* Adaptation requires a population of ideas and practices, from which the fittest ones can be selected. An organization adapting to a changing environment is the result of experimentation at the level of the individual. Adaptation is not therefore primarily a cultural attribute or a policy, but rather the individual will and freedom to try new things.

Organizations need to overcome these tendencies and false beliefs in order to achieve adaptation. They must embrace trial-and-error, which necessarily means some initiatives will fail. Executives must establish the organizational context, not issue the instruction set. The front line must be empowered, individually. There must be a bias to action. The substance of adaptation must be understood an embraced. We must overcome our obsession with efficiency and overly cautious "practicality." Imagination should be embraced. And we must reconcile the apparent contradiction between divergence and convergence.

None of these imperatives are new. What needs to change to unlock adaptation are the false beliefs underpinning them.

Martin Reeves, Thijs Venema, and Claire Love
Chapter 7
Shaping to Win

Have you heard of Sir Hiram Maxim, inventor of the light bulb? Maxim is, in fact, one of a host of inventors who, along with Thomas Edison, could be credited with developing the first viable technology. Yet Edison's is the name universally linked to the invention. Why?

Edison's light bulb would ultimately prove technically superior to those designed by his contemporaries. But the main reason Edison's name is forever associated with the light bulb is his ability to successfully *shape the environment necessary to commercialize his invention.* At the first public demonstration of his bulb in Menlo Park in 1879, Edison proclaimed, "We will make electricity so cheap that only the rich will burn candles." Only two years later, he switched on his company's first power station, in lower Manhattan. Within five years, Edison's distribution network numbered more than 120 stations, backed by supporting Edison inventions such as the Edison Jumbo generator, the Edison electrical feeder, and parallel distribution.

But Edison did not limit his shaping activities to the physical domain. He also worked to conquer the hearts and minds of stakeholders. When alternating-current technology challenged the direct-current technology on which his distribution system depended, for example, Edison unleashed a publicity campaign to convince the public and regulators that the new technology was unsafe.

More than a century later, companies are deploying similarly powerful shaping strategies to take advantage of profound shifts occurring in many industries, sectors, and regions. Global health-care company Novo Nordisk, for example, engaged regulators, doctors, and patients to shape the Chinese diabetes-care market to the company's advantage. Facebook opened its platform to outside developers – and leveraged the resulting ecosystem to overtake its competition. Southwest Airlines successfully reshaped a mature market by unleashing its own disruptive innovation.

Like Edison, these companies understood that the unpredictable but malleable environment in which they operated required a shaping strategy. Let's explore how they did this in seemingly very different markets.

https://doi.org/10.1515/9783110755381-007

The Shaping Imperative

What we did initially, which is what we do everywhere in the world, is to start building a relationship with the government, explaining to them about diabetes, the problems they have, and starting to educate the whole public-health sector. To date, we have educated maybe 50,000 to 60,000 physicians in China about diabetes. So you could say our marketing in China has been education.[1]

– Lars Rebien Sørensen, CEO, Novo Nordisk

Shaping is one of five fundamentally distinct strategy styles or approaches to strategy. Like the others – *classical, adaptive, visionary,* and *survival* – it is suited to specific market environments.[2] A company's choice of style should ultimately be driven by three factors: a market's (1) unpredictability, (2) malleability (that is, the degree to which a company can influence competitive forces), and (3) harshness.

Conditions in many markets today lend themselves to shaping strategies. Unpredictability is rising, driven by globalization, ongoing advances in technology, increased transparency, and other factors. Simultaneously, many markets are becoming more malleable. High growth rates and fragmentation in new markets create opportunities to deploy new business models. Technological change creates opportunities for disruptive innovation. Demographic shifts create new markets whose development can be influenced. As governments wrestle with these dynamics, there is also potential for companies to shape regulation.

Three arenas are particularly suited to shaping strategies: (1) emerging markets; (2) young, dynamic industries; and (3) mature industries ripe for disruption (Figure 7.1).

Emerging Markets

Our analysis suggests that emerging markets are fully twice as unpredictable and malleable as mature ones.[3] Their unpredictability is spawned by a host of factors, including these economies' high dependence on exports and foreign direct investment, as well as vulnerability to fluctuations in commodity prices

---

1 "Interview with Lars Rebien Sørensen, CEO, Novo Nordisk," *Pharma Boardroom*, April 30, 2013, https://pharmaboardroom.com/interviews/interview-with-lars-rebien-s-rensen-president-ceo-novo-nordisk/.
2 For a full discussion of these styles, see "Your Strategy Needs a Strategy," BCG article, October 2012, https://www.bcg.com/publications/2012/your-strategy-needs-a-strategy.
3 We measured uncertainty using market capitalization volatility, and we measured malleability using a composite index of growth, returns to scale, and industry fragmentation.

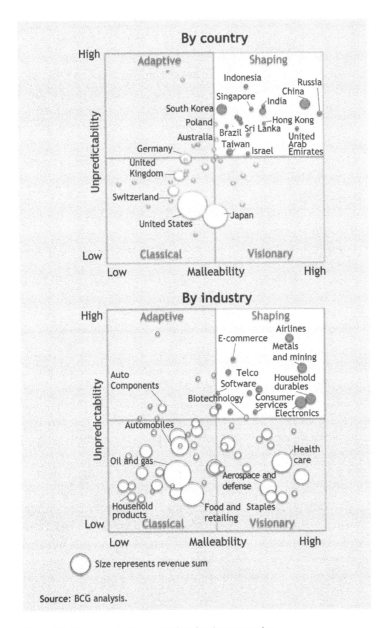

Figure 7.1: Many markets are ripe for shaping strategies.

and exchange rates. At the same time, these markets are uniquely malleable, given their high growth rates, fragmented industries, shifting demographics, and evolving regulation.

Novo Nordisk seized such opportunities when it moved to shape the Chinese diabetes market starting in the 1990s, well before the scale of the threat of diabetes in China was widely appreciated. The company's efforts were multi-pronged. It invested in physician education, created an advisory board of key opinion leaders, and raised awareness through policy forums and other events. Novo's engagement earned it a seat at the table with policymakers, which helped the company drive the development of nationwide clinical treatment guidelines for diabetes and patient education.

Novo's shaping of its environment formed a strong underpinning for growth. By 2010, the company had a greater than 60 percent share of China's insulin market and roughly 35 percent of the country's total diabetes-care market, double that of its nearest competitor.

Young, Dynamic Industries

These industries, such as software and Internet services, offer a similarly significant upside to those bold enough to shape them. Young, dynamic industries are intrinsically unpredictable: no one could have forecast with any accuracy the size, growth rate, and profitability of the markets created by the iPhone, Facebook, and fracking. Such industries are generally malleable, too: barriers to entry are low, products are new to regulators, and it is unclear which companies and business models will come out on top.

Facebook is a prime example of a company that shaped a young, dynamic industry. One of its smartest moves was to open its platform to outside developers in 2007, thus attracting all manner of applications. The company could not hope to predict how big or successful any given app would become – but it did not need to. By 2008, it had attracted 33,000 applications; by 2010, that number had risen to more than 550,000.

As the industry developed, and more than two-thirds of the successful social-networking apps turned out to be games, it was not surprising that the most popular ones resided on Facebook. Even if the social-networking landscape were to shift dramatically, chances are, by virtue of pure numbers, that the most popular applications will still be on Facebook. By creating a flexible, popular platform, the company actively shaped the environment to its advantage – rather than merely staking out a position in an existing market or reacting to changes after they occurred.

Mature Industries Ripe for Disruption

Many mature, seemingly staid industries can also be ideally suited to shaping strategies. Unpredictability can flare up in these markets, and low growth and limited innovation can force companies to find new revenue models. Dissatisfied customers may become hungry for alternative products and services. Mature industries can also become malleable, particularly if the industry experiences sudden changes in regulation or technology, which can weaken incumbents.

Take airlines as an example. By the 1980s, the industry had become a low-growth, relatively fragmented market. Southwest Airlines shook the industry with the launch of a disruptively innovative business model centered on low costs, no-frills service, quick turnarounds, and point-to-point flights. The model was the basis for Southwest's shaping strategy, which took incumbents by surprise and shifted the basis of competition.

Southwest complemented this by successfully leveraging a broad range of stakeholders. It forged mutually beneficial relations with secondary airports, allowing it to bypass hubs dominated by established airlines. It actively involved itself in local economies, giving the company a seat at the table with policymakers. This has been a winning strategy. Southwest has inspired a generation of low-cost airlines.

Shape Up!

Successful market shapers such as Novo Nordisk, Facebook, and Southwest Airlines demonstrate a number of critical capabilities that aspiring shapers must embrace and develop. Foremost among them are the following:

- *Recognize the opportunity.* Companies must determine whether their market is indeed ripe for shaping based on its unpredictability and malleability. Unpredictability can be gauged by volatility in market capitalization, demand, profitability, and competitive positioning. Malleability can be assessed through growth rates, returns to scale, industry fragmentation, and ripeness for disruption.
- *Deal with unpredictability.* Environments that can be shaped are rife with uncertainty. To negotiate this, companies must employ several adaptive behaviors. First, they must continuously scan the environment, recognize changing dynamics, and respond in real time. Second, they must ensure that their organization has sufficient flexibility through a modular structure that fosters collaboration and experimentation, supported by leadership that values risk

taking and is open to ideas from outside the company. Third, companies must experiment continuously, since predicting which products or strategies will be successful can be difficult.

– *Influence stakeholders.* Companies must influence stakeholders through intimacy, collaboration, and advocacy; and strive to develop close relationships with key opinion leaders and decision makers, working to understand their motivations. Companies need to demonstrate that they are acting not just in their own narrow interests but in the interests of all stakeholders.

– *Demonstrate commitment.* Companies must walk the talk. Advocacy alone is not enough; a business that aspires to shape a market must show credible commitment through investment and transparency.

– *Develop an ecosystem.* Once stakeholders are convinced and commitments have been made, a company can accelerate change by building a multicompany ecosystem. The company should design incentives that turn the arrangement into a win-win for all participants. It should also take steps to orchestrate collaboration among participants when necessary and ensure sufficient diversity and depth of partners. It should endeavor to create an environment in which transparency and feedback drive collective learning.

– *Innovate disruptively.* Finally, would-be shapers should seek to leverage disruptive innovation by redefining their business model after looking externally and asking if there are customer needs that could be solved better or differently. Disruptive innovation, such as the launch of Apple's iPhone, can play a substantial role in shaping an environment – and make a company a very attractive partner.

In today's increasingly turbulent business world, shaping strategies stand to become ever more necessary and valuable. Companies that fail to recognize the opportunity and seize the moment to shape their circumstances risk being shaped by them.

Martin Reeves, Julien Legrand, and Jack Fuller
Chapter 8
Your Strategy Process Needs a Strategy

Since the birth of business strategy as a discipline in the early 1960s, business leaders have had access to an ever wider range of approaches to strategy: the classical plan-and-execute approach, adaptive strategy, ecosystem-based strategy, blue ocean strategy,[1] value migration, the dynamic capabilities approach, and so on.[2]

But despite this broadening array of approaches, the process of developing and realizing strategy within a company has remained essentially the same: strategic planning. Senior executives supply an ambition and direction, business units develop a more detailed plan grounded in market and competitive analysis, and the plan is challenged, finalized, and adopted until the next planning cycle. The problem is, there can be a dramatic mismatch between this process and the business environment. Fast-changing conditions can quickly make any plan obsolete. For instance, a company may need to be more experimental and exploratory, or to co-evolve with other actors in a multicompany ecosystem, neither of which is facilitated by episodic, company-wide planning cycles.

We need to rethink the *process* by which we define and operationalize strategy. We need to widen the process options available to the strategy function, so that our strategy truly helps us win in the specific business environment we are facing.

The Challenges of Different Environments

As business environments have grown more diverse in recent decades, picking the right approach to strategy for each context has become increasingly important. As shown in Figure 8.1, there are five broad approaches to strategy:

---

1 https://www.blueoceanstrategy.com/what-is-blue-ocean-strategy/.

2 For more on the various approaches to strategy, and for the context of many of the quotations used in this article, see Martin Reeves, Knut Haanaes, and Janmejaya Sinha, *Your Strategy Needs a Strategy: How to Choose and Execute the Right Approach*, Harvard Business Review Press, 2015, https://store.hbr.org/product/your-strategy-needs-a-strategy-how-to-choose-and-execute-the-right-approach/14054?sku=14054-HBK-ENG.

https://doi.org/10.1515/9783110755381-008

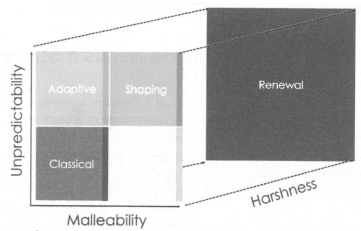

Source: For more on the various approaches to strategy, and for the context of many of the references used in this article, see Martin Reeves, Knut Haanaes, and Janmejaya Sinha, *Your Strategy Needs a Strategy: How to Choose and Execute the Right Approach,* Harvard Business Review Press, 2015.

Figure 8.1: Five broad approaches to strategy.

1. *Classical:* clear phases of analysis, planning, and execution; useful in predictable and stable contexts, such as mature categories that grow with GDP (confectionary and cosmetics, for example)
2. *Adaptive:* continual experimentation and scaling up of what works; useful in unpredictable environments in which new technologies or business models drive changing offerings and patterns of demand
3. *Visionary:* use of imagination to create a game-changing product, service, or business model, followed by persistence in the creation and development of a market; useful when a firm can have a significant influence over the environment rather than merely adapting to it
4. *Shaping:* collaboration in environments that are simultaneously unpredictable and malleable, requiring companies to leverage ecosystems and platforms
5. *Renewal:* execution of necessary, radical moves when the environment is harsh or there has been a protracted mismatch between the firm's strategy and its environment, with limited time and resources to analyze and deliberate a course of action

A leader needs to get three things right when it comes to strategy: (1) read the business environment correctly, (2) choose a general approach to strategy that fits the environment, then (3) set up a process to enact that approach in her particular company. Even if an executive gets the first two parts right and identifies the right approach – renewal, say – the company may end up sticking with classical, firm-wide cycles of planning or setting up multiple experiments – processes that are too slow or not radical enough for a renewal strategy. And so the initial, insightful intention – the chosen approach – is not realized in practice.

Linking up the approach and the process is not easy. When General Electric set out to become a leading digital company around 2011, for example, then-CEO Jeff Immelt was aware of the need for an adaptive approach. As he noted, "One of the hardest challenges in driving change is allowing new information to come in constantly and giving yourself the chance to adapt." That approach, however, was in some ways at odds with the way GE actually developed and operationalized its particular strategy. Backed by large investments, it set out a major vision: to create the "operating system for the industrial internet."[3] As Immelt reported, "We have hired thousands of people and invested billions in technology." According to interviews with GE managers, these moves ran up against the fast-changing IoT environment, which, as Immelt suggested, did require adaptability, even from a company with GE's resources. GE shifted course, focusing on experimenting with industrial apps for existing customers – a process that fits with an adaptive, "test and scale" approach.

GE's example demonstrates the importance of coherence not only between the market reality and the broad approach to strategy, but also between these and the process for developing and realizing the company's particular strategy.

Five Approaches to Strategy

Let's consider the processes best suited to different approaches to strategy. For each of the five approaches outlined above, we can define a matching process.

Classical Approach: Planning

The essence of the classical approach is to create and implement a stable plan of action, which works best when the environment is relatively predictable. The job of the process, then, is to enable the creation of an *actionable plan*.

---

3 https://www.nytimes.com/2018/04/19/business/ge-digital-ambitions.html.

The initial direction or ambition comes from the executive team. This is usually followed by various kinds of analysis, like market modeling (projecting category growth and future share) and detailed financial forecasting. This process takes some time because ideas have to be analytically verified and consolidated, with the final call made by the executive team. An example is the strategy process in the core business of Mars. As past president Paul Michaels noted, "We plan because we operate in relatively stable markets." After consultation, plans are set from the top by a small group: "It's me, the CFO, and a few others."

We can represent this planning process with the letter v. That is, starting from the top left of the v, the executive team sends the initial direction down to the business units (the bottom of the v), which send elaborated plans back to corporate, which finalizes the plan.

Adaptive Approach: Experimentation

In less predictable environments, centralized cycles of planning make less sense. Instead, the strategic approach is to experiment and adapt rapidly to exploit unpredictably changing conditions. Here then, the process is about facilitating and capitalizing on experimentation.

This works best when experimentation happens in short cycles of testing and picking winners. Key ingredients of the process are the ability to collect and read signals to detect business opportunities; free flow of data throughout the company, enabling teams to identify opportunities with little central supervision; and the culture and organizational mechanisms to enable failures to be easily discontinued and successes to be scaled.

Zara enacts its adaptive strategy in this way, identifying emerging trends via real-time market experiments with its clothing styles and making small commitments – only 15% to 25% of a season's line is set six months in advance – that can quickly be scaled up. This process can be captured by the letter o, to represent short, iterative cycles of testing and identifying opportunities.

Visionary Approach: Imagination

A visionary approach works when the market is malleable to a particular company, so that rather than simply responding to given conditions, the company can create or shape a market around a transformative offering. In this case, the job of the process is to facilitate imagination, home in on a visionary product, service, or business model, and then persist resourcefully to drive it into the market.

Imagination works in iterative cycles, taking a starting point – often a desire, or a frustration that a need is not being met – and elaborating it into a worked-out proposal or prototype. In popular stories of imagination, like that of Steve Jobs, this process is assumed to occur in the head of one person. But in fact it is a social process. At Apple, Steve Jobs elaborated his ideas by iterating with Jony Ive and others. To take another example, the concept behind 23andMe was formulated over time by Anne Wojcicki, drawing on her experience in health care and refined in discussions with scientists and engineers.

Key ingredients of this process are the richness of mental models brought to bear on the initial ideas; a willingness to be patient with ideas still in formation; effective learning from prototypes; and a determination to persist until a market has been created. It can be represented by the letter q, with the circular portion standing for imaginative iteration within the company. Then, once the visionary product has been created, it must be driven to market: the tail of the q.

Shaping Approach: Collaboration

When an environment is malleable yet unpredictable – meaning it would be unwise to commit to a long-term visionary effort – an ecosystem or platform-based approach is appropriate. The strategy process here is about supporting effective collaboration to shape an unpredictable environment to the advantage of the company and others whose interests coincide.

Alibaba[4] has done this exceptionally well, building a popular platform, engaging others, and shaping the direction of e-commerce in China. Another example is Red Hat, which creates open-source software by engaging a community of programmers. Success with this process requires building a platform to coordinate collaboration and co-evolving the offering in concert with other actors. It also requires building a highly responsive organization; Alibaba leads here, aiming to become a self-tuning organization,[5] with "as many operating decisions as possible made by machines fueled by live data" drawn from its ecosystem.

We can represent this process with a capital O. Like the adaptive, experimental process (represented by the lower-case o), the collaborative process involves cycles of testing, learning, and evolving the firm's ideas and tactics.

---

4 https://hbr.org/2018/09/alibaba-and-the-future-of-business.
5 https://hbr.org/2015/06/the-self-tuning-enterprise.

However, the larger size of the *O* signifies that the process encompasses actors beyond the bounds of the company.

Renewal Approach: Pragmatism

When the environment becomes so harsh that the company's viability is threatened, immediate corrective actions are required. The job of the strategy process here is to facilitate fast interventions; it involves making pragmatic choices under pressure to find a path back to growth.

We can represent this process by *I*, indicating top-down, fast decision making that aims to ensure survival. Doing this well is difficult, as time and, therefore, the quality of information may be limited. There is little scope for comprehensive analysis or engagement, internally or externally. Rather, a few critical turnaround initiatives must be driven from the top. An example is American Express in the harsh environment from 2008 to 2009. "First we had to deal with the cost issue . . . we had to act immediately," explained then-CEO Ken Chenault, emphasizing the need to analyze the firm's cost structure as a basis for quick cost-saving decisions, followed by "selectively investing in growth."

Customizing Strategy Processes

The five strategy processes described above are really points on a continuum. We should also consider how they can be combined into variations appropriate to different circumstances.

Two commonly employed variants illustrate this idea: *v* (the planning process) is often extended to become a *w*, indicating further rounds of iteration between corporate leadership and the business units. Similarly, *v* (the planning process) and *o* (the experimentation process) are often combined to form *vo*, meaning an initial exercise to define some guiding principles followed by continual reassessment as the company learns what works and what doesn't.

Many other variations are possible. For example: multiple programs of experimentation run in a persistently unpredictable environment (*oo*); initial ecosystem engagement setting the direction for subsequent adaptive experimentation (*Oo*); an initial phase of experimentation informing an imaginative, visionary effort (*oq*). Figure 8.2 shows the different "tints" and "shades" available in the palette of strategy processes.

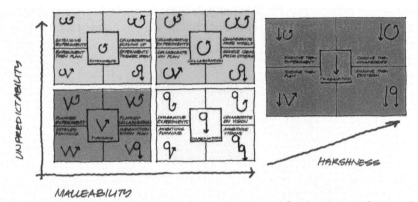

MALLEABILITY

Source: For more on the various approaches to strategy, and for the context of many of the references used in this article, see Martin Reeves, Knut Haanaes, and Janmejaya Sinha, *Your Strategy Needs a Strategy: How to Choose and Execute the Right Approach,* Harvard Business Review Press, 2015.

Figure 8.2: Variations in strategy processes.

Managing Multiple Strategy Processes

The majority of companies employ a single strategy process – usually classical planning – rolled out uniformly. But a large company almost always faces multiple business environments, across time or simultaneously in different parts of the company. Environments that are more or less predictable and malleable require different strategic approaches, each enacted via a suitable process. Thus, business leaders and strategy departments need to be able to manage multiple variants of strategy processes.

Like someone working with both hands at once, an "ambidextrous" business[6] can deploy different strategic approaches across business units – one unit taking a classical approach and another taking an adaptive approach, for example. Such businesses need ambidexterity in processes, too, meaning that the different strategic approaches need to be successfully operationalized.

Leaders of such ambidextrous businesses need to define "metaprocesses," that is, a way of orchestrating different strategy processes across a complex firm. How this should be done depends on *diversity* (the variety of business

---

6 https://www.bcg.com/publications/2013/strategy-growth-ambidexterity-art-thriving-complex-environments.

environments the company faces) and *dynamism* (the frequency of change in those environments). Along these dimensions we can define four such meta-processes (Figure 8.3).

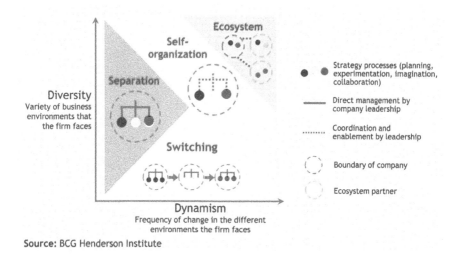

Source: BCG Henderson Institute

Figure 8.3: Metaprocesses within strategy processes.

1. *High Diversity, Low Dynamism: Separation:* When the diversity of environments is high (the business faces many types of environment at once) but dynamism is low (the set of environments stays the same), it makes sense to run separate strategy processes in parallel, overseen by corporate leadership.

    This requires leaders to be familiar with a range of approaches to strategy and the processes needed to enact them. They should be aware of the different demands of each process and its expected outputs: annual plans from a classical unit, plausibly transformative ideas from a visionary unit, and so on. Former CEO of PepsiCo, Indra Nooyi, has described this kind of separation: "The team that runs the core business should keep doing what they're doing efficiently . . . the other teams should not be motivated by the current model but focus totally on disrupting it."

2. *Low Diversity, High Dynamism: Switching:* When diversity is low but dynamism is high (the firm faces just one type of environment, say, but it changes over time), it makes sense to switch processes along with major shifts in the business context. This requires business leaders to regularly reassess the

environment and be ready to change the strategy process as needed – even if this involves disruptive top-down interventions in existing ways of working. ING Bank Netherlands did this successfully, switching from a classical to an adaptive, "agile," approach as the relatively stable banking environment was disrupted and became less predictable.

3. *High Diversity, High Dynamism: Self-Organization:* In diverse and dynamic situations, top-down management becomes too complex to be tenable. The executive team should instead leave room for business units to self-organize, determining the most suitable strategy process given the environment that each faces at any given time. Corporate still has a role to play, though, in creating the "internal market" for resources and the rules that regulate its operation.

    Consumer electronics company Haier developed such a model, aiming to build an "enterprise . . . able to operate by itself with employees acting as their own leaders." It organized the company into 2,000 largely self-governing units, while the CEO aimed to become "a leader whose existence is unknown to his subordinates."

4. *Very High Diversity and Dynamism: Indirect Influence:* In the most diverse and dynamic situations, a firm may not be able to pursue the full suite of required processes internally and instead need to orchestrate an ecosystem, or multiple ecosystems, of external partners. In this case, leaders must do what they can to shape the ecosystem favorably, while collaborating with partners who may be running very different strategy processes. This is often achieved indirectly via a digital platform, such as a two-sided marketplace. For example, Apple has a visionary process for many of its products, while within its app store, many companies run experimental, adaptive processes; at the same time, Apple collaborates with manufacturers that face comparatively predictable environments and employ classical strategy processes. There is no way that Apple alone could exploit the full range of environments across its ecosystem; it would be impossible to manage the entire app store and all of Apple's other partners as departments of one company. But Apple profits by collaborating with multiple companies running different strategy processes.

Reinventing the Strategy Function

Adopting multiple approaches and processes simultaneously requires a reconception of the role of the strategy department. As the guardian of strategy, the strategy function should aim to move the organization away from a monolithic approach and toward an ambidextrous approach – developing the ability to implement a variety of strategy processes. The actions required to achieve this are:

- *Educate the company.* Ensure that everyone understands both the need for multiple approaches to strategy and the processes required to operationalize them.
- *Set the tone with the right questions.* The different processes are also defined by different questions: each signals a different way of thinking and acting appropriate to the chosen strategic approach.
- *Build the needed capabilities.* Hire, deploy, and cultivate talent able to work with different approaches to strategy, and provide the tools (frameworks, exercises, games) required to develop those strategies.
- *Determine the right mix of strategy approaches.* Company strategists should monitor the environments in which the company operates and identify the approaches and processes best suited to each situation.
- *Choose the right metaprocess.* Determining the way to manage multiple strategy processes at once is a critical task for the strategy team and senior executives.
- *Be a change agent.* Ensure that the company does not stick with processes maladapted to the environment(s) it faces.
- *Govern strategy effectively.* Develop a process library, that is, guidelines for business units or the firm as a whole in choosing the right strategic approach and the process for carrying it out.

Two companies that have achieved these goals are Mahindra and Alibaba.

Mahindra refers to itself as a federation of businesses, educating its leaders to be orchestrators "sensitive to the different pieces and how they flow together." The Strategy Group operates several types of strategy "war rooms" that study trends and challenges, budget questions, and operations, employing an 11-question framework designed to challenge and strengthen business unit strategies. It orchestrates process variation across the company according to each business unit's stage of development in its market. For units facing classical environments, the central team "drills down into incredible detail" on the unit's plans, while emphasizing the need for feedback loops in younger, more experimental businesses.

As described by its CSO, Ming Zeng, in his recent book, Alibaba aims to be a "self-tuning enterprise." "Embrace change" is a core tenet of Jack Ma's leadership; the company educates its leaders by means of frequent rotations among business units.[7] Units have a high degree of autonomy and the ability to run their own experiments. The central Alibaba planning process leaves space for this: plans are written as starting points rather than ends in themselves, and business unit leaders are allowed to explore new directions. Finally, when change is needed but difficult, Alibaba still has the ability to initiate tightly executed programs from the top, best illustrated by the significant number of reorganizations the company has gone through over the course of its growth.

Even for those leaders who understand that varied approaches to strategy are required, it can be difficult to realize these organizationally. Companies are often stuck with a classical plan-and-execute process that is as much an embedded mindset as a set of collective routines. To best take advantage of each environment a firm faces, we need to actively consider the right strategic approaches and enact these effectively by adopting the right processes.

7 Ming Zeng, *Smart Business: What Alibaba's Success Reveals About the Future of Strategy*, Harvard Business Review Press, 2018.

Martin Reeves, Frida Polli, TejPavan Gandhok, Lewis Baker, Hen Lotan, and Julien Legrand

Chapter 9
Your Capabilities Need a Strategy: Choosing and Developing the Right Ones for Each Environment

Businesses today are competing in an increasingly diverse set of environments: across multiple dimensions, the range of conditions faced by different businesses has increased dramatically since the 1980s.[1] Strategy cannot be one-size-fits-all: to succeed today, leaders must understand how to match their approach to strategy and implementation to the specific environment for each business.

As shown in Chapter 8, "Your Strategy Process Needs a Strategy," there are five distinct business environments, each of which requires its own approach to strategy and execution – classical, adaptive, visionary, shaping, and renewal.

Once an organization has identified the right conceptual approach to strategy, it needs to understand which capabilities are required in order to execute the approach, and how these can be identified. One way to do so is by leveraging the power of games[2] to measure and develop skills consistently and cost effectively.[3] By using games designed to measure performance and behavior in different settings, in combination with artificial intelligence and theories from neuroscience, businesses can identify and develop the right leadership for each strategic environment.

To understand the power of a games-driven approach and identify the traits that best predict success in different environments, the BCG Henderson Institute, pymetrics,[4] and Professor TejPavan Gandhok (one of the authors of this article) from the Indian School of Business collaborated to study the strategy skills and neuroscience profiles of about 360 strategists with diverse backgrounds across different regions. We found that different cognitive and emotional traits (also known as cognitive neuroscience measures) reliably predict success in different simulated business environments, and that only a few individuals were

---

1 Based on range of market cap volatility and revenue growth by company; see introduction to *Your Strategy Needs a Strategy*.
2 https://www.bcg.com/publications/2018/strategy-games-mind.
3 https://www.bcg.com/industries/public-sector/future-skills-architect-tool.
4 https://www.pymetrics.ai/science.

https://doi.org/10.1515/9783110755381-009

able to perform well across all environments. This demonstrates that what it takes to be a good strategist is highly context-dependent – so companies must understand the strategy skills they need for each environment, develop the right talent base, and take a data-driven approach to talent management and development.

Different Neuroscience Measures for Different Environments

Our study of strategy skills and cognitive and emotional traits is drawn from two sets of games. In strategy games[5] developed by the BCG Henderson Institute, players operate a virtual "lemonade stand" while facing conditions that simulate one of the five types of business environment. Players are scored on how well they can deploy the right skills for each environment (for example, analysis and planning in the classical environment, or experimentation in the adaptive environment).

Our study of cognitive neuroscience measures is based on a series of games developed by pymetrics. In these games, players undertake challenges that test their underlying cognitive or emotional traits (for example, attempting to fill a virtual balloon up to just before its breaking point as a test of risk aversion). Players are assessed on 91 cognitive neuroscience measures based on their actions in each game (see Box 9.1)

Box 9.1: Using Strategy and Neuroscience Games to Assess Strategy Skills

The BCG Henderson Institute developed a strategy game for its clients and consultants to understand the range of strategic environments and the approach required to succeed in them. Players compete against "Bruce Henderson" to operate a lemonade stand in different business environments, aiming to generate more profits than Bruce. In order to win, players need to deploy the right strategy approach for each environment.

For example, in the Adaptive environment, clouds appear randomly above crowds, which then disperse, resulting in lower foot traffic in the area. Players thus need to continuously pay attention to changing conditions and adapt their actions accordingly. Across all environments, players' actions – such as scouting new locations and choosing how often to move and when to grow – are tracked, scored, and analyzed.

Pymetrics deploys a series of neuroscience-based games to measure individuals' cognitive and emotional traits ("cognitive neuroscience measures"). Participants play a number of mini-games to this end. A variety of actions, such as speed of reaction or number of right or wrong

---

5 https://hbr.org/2015/09/games-can-make-you-a-better-strategist.

answers, are tracked and analyzed using pymetrics' proprietary algorithms to quantify the player's cognitive neuroscience measures.

For example, in one mini-game, participants are invited to use a pump to inflate a virtual balloon. Each pump earns them money. The choice to pump more and earn more money, however, comes with the risk of popping the balloon and losing everything. Each moment therefore offers the choice between stopping and collecting the money, or further inflating the balloon. Players' decisions in this game indicate their risk affinity, and the total amount of money they collect indicates their performance when facing risky situations.

By collecting each player's scores on both sets of games, we built a unique dataset combining strategists' cognitive neuroscience measures and strategy skills. Using multiple regression analysis, we identified the cognitive neuroscience measures that were most correlated with success in each type of strategy environment. We found that certain traits were reliable signals of strategy skills – but importantly, the traits needed to succeed were different across environments. Below we describe some of the most prominent traits to demonstrate how they contribute to success in the different strategic environments. The full list of statistically significant traits is included in Figure 9.2.

In classical environments, the most important traits include:

- *Detail-oriented:* adept at collecting, gathering, visualizing, and analyzing information in detail.
- *Good at planning:* excels at developing a structured plan by laying out specific steps towards a goal.
- *Focused:* able to filter out noise and maintain attention on specific tasks.

In predictable and stable environments, the ideal approach to strategy involves analyzing key drivers of performance and executing a plan to address them. It is not surprising that the best strategists in such environments are able to conduct detailed analysis, create logical plans, and remain focused on them.

The most important traits in adaptive environments include:

- *Good at multitasking:* capable of handling several tasks simultaneously.
- *Quick to evaluate opportunities:* able to assess situations quickly.
- *Open to trial-and-error:* willing to try different actions despite understanding that failure may occur.

In more unpredictable environments, strategists must be able to manage a portfolio of bets. As new opportunities emerge and new information about them is revealed, effective strategists quickly select and scale the successful ones in a process of trial and error.

The most important traits in visionary environments include:
- *Good memory:* strong ability to recall details of past experiences.
- *Self-assured:* confident in one's statements and actions.
- *Self-critical:* frequently questioning and re-evaluating one's behavior.

In predictable and malleable environments, strategists must envision new possibilities, which may build upon past experiences. Then they must build the company to make that vision a reality, which requires a balance of self-assurance to persist with the vision as well as self-criticism to question when a change of tactics is necessary to achieve it.

The most important traits in shaping environments include:
- *Reciprocal:* willing to give as well as to take.
- *Deliberate:* acts consciously and intentionally.
- *At ease with ambiguity:* able to act and decide on partial information.

Unpredictable and malleable environments require mutual trust and reciprocity among stakeholders. Though the foundation for productive ecosystems must be laid carefully and deliberately, ecosystems evolve organically, requiring strategists to be comfortable with the ambiguity that comes from having only partial control.

The most important traits in renewal environments include:
- *Resilient:* able to withstand difficult conditions.
- *Quick to execute:* swift in driving decisions into actions.
- *Motivated by larger rewards:* filters out low-value opportunities.

Harsh environments and circumstances require strategists to be resilient in order to maintain their focus in the face of a crisis. Bold, pragmatic moves are often required to restore viability, and speed of action can make the difference between success and failure. Together, these sets of traits demonstrate the skills palette that businesses need to paint with in order to set and execute strategy effectively (Figure 9.1). The optimal skills for strategists vary significantly across each environment.

Ambidexterity is Rare but can be Achieved

As the business world becomes more diverse, not only are companies more likely to face changing strategic environments over time, but they may face multiple environments simultaneously. Therefore, the ideal strategists must not

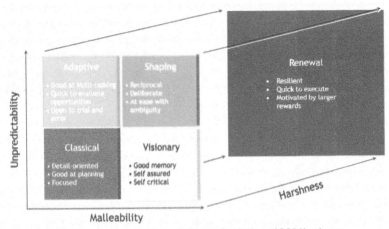

Source: Data collected by pymetrics, Professor TejPavan Gandhok, and BCG Henderson
Institute: analysis by pymetrics and BCG Henderson Institute

Figure 9.1: The sets of traits needed to set and execute strategy effectively.

only have the skills to succeed in one environment, but they must be able to
master multiple ones – in other words, they must be *ambidextrous*.

However, truly ambidextrous strategists are quite scarce, comprising about
2% of the population that we studied.[6] (Coincidentally, previous BCG research
found that roughly the same share of companies are ambidextrous.[7]) While
businesses might have historically conceived of the "strategist" as a singular ar-
chetype, our results show that, in reality, most strategists have distinct profiles
and strengths, allowing them to excel in specific strategic contexts.

As for each of the five strategic environments individually, we analyzed the
cognitive neuroscience measures that were most common among the most ambidextrous strategists. Not surprisingly, the profile of ambidextrous strategists
combines traits that were important in each environment, including being good
at planning, open to trial-and-error, self-critical, deliberate, and self-assured
(Figure 9.2).

---

6 Individuals were considered ambidextrous if they earned above 80% of the maximum score
in all five business environments.
7 https://www.bcg.com/publications/2018/2-percent-company .

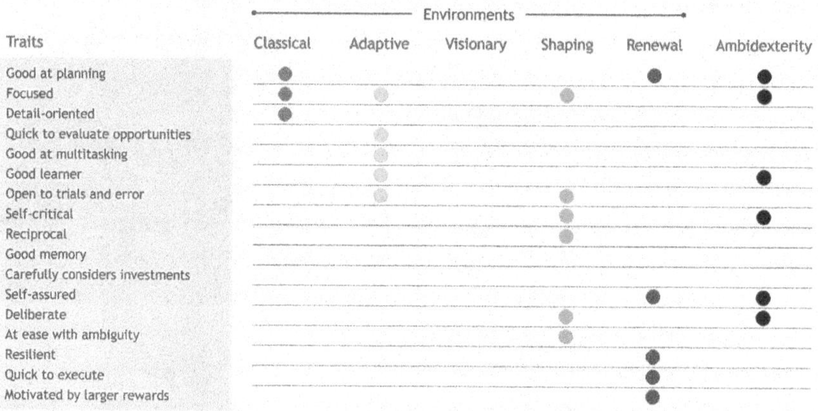

Traits	Classical	Adaptive	Visionary	Shaping	Renewal	Ambidexterity
			Environments			
Good at planning	●				●	●
Focused	●	○		○		●
Detail-oriented	●					
Quick to evaluate opportunities			○			
Good at multitasking			○			
Good learner			○			●
Open to trials and error		○				●
Self-critical				●		●
Reciprocal				●		
Good memory						
Carefully considers investments						
Self-assured					●	●
Deliberate				○		●
At ease with ambiguity				○		
Resilient					●	
Quick to execute					●	
Motivated by larger rewards					●	

Source: Data collected by pymetrics, Professor TejPavan Gandhok, and BCG Henderson Institute; analysis by pymetrics and BCG Henderson Institute.
Note: Interpretation of significant traits across all environments, based on combined datasets.

Figure 9.2: The five strategic environments and traits for success.

The Limits of Traditional Personality Tests

Many organizations today use personality tests to analyze individuals' preferences, characteristics, and behaviors, with the goal of assessing their fit within a team or company. Plausibly, these psychological profiles could also be used to assess how strategists' skills and capabilities match their roles. But personality tests differ considerably from cognitive neuroscience measures, both in the traits measured and in the method of measurement. The data derived from cognitive neuroscience instruments comes from measuring objective behavior, whereas traditional personality tests measure self-report of higher-level phenomena.

To test if personality traits are also useful for determining strategy skills, we evaluated participants on two prominent personality profiles – the Big Five and the Rational Experiential Inventory.[8] Once again, we used regression analysis to determine the correlation of each personality trait to scores in the five environments of the strategy game.

We found that, unlike the cognitive neuroscience measures, the personality traits of the Big Five and REI did *not* consistently predict strategy skills. Our findings indicate that the innate, deeply coded nature of cognitive neuroscience

---

8 The Big Five describes individuals' openness to experience, conscientiousness, extraversion, agreeableness, and neuroticism; the REI compares recourse to intuition vs. to logic.

measures is more relevant when it comes to making and acting on the strategic decisions that are necessary for success in each of the five environments.

All Strategic Approaches can be Learned, but at Different Rates

If particular skills are required to succeed in each business environment, can companies develop these capabilities by training strategists to be well-rounded? The answer depends on whether or not strategy skills can be learned, and how effectively. To understand how well each approach can be learned, we measured the rate at which participants' scores improved on repeated iterations of the strategy game in each environment.

We found that all approaches can be learned, but at very different rates (Figure 9.3). The strategy skills required to succeed in classical and renewal environments were learned relatively quickly: In those environments, players' scores increased by an average of 15% and 13%, respectively, in their first ten games. In contrast, the skills required to succeed in visionary, adaptive, and shaping environments were much more challenging to improve through practice. Mastering ambidexterity was the most challenging, with an average learning rate of roughly 1% during the first ten games played in each environment.

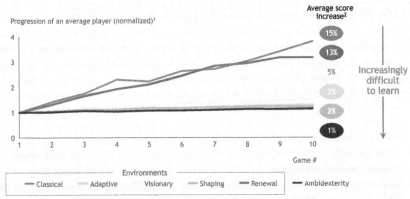

Sources: Data collected by pymetrics, Professor TejPavan Gandhok, and BCG Henderson Institute; analysis by pymetrics and BCG Henderson Institute.
[1]Normalized score calculated on the basis of average increase between two successive rounds.
[1]Average across ten games.

Figure 9.3: All approaches can be learned, but at different rates.

The difference in learning rates reflects the intrinsic difficulty of decision making in each environment. Classical and renewal have a relatively well-defined set of levers to drive strategy and execution. Classical environments are stable, so the levers required to win tomorrow can be predicted from analyzing those that worked yesterday; similarly, given the imminent threat to survival in renewal environments, the initial key success driver is a single-minded focus on rapidly restoring viability through enhanced efficiency.

In contrast, adaptive, visionary, and shaping environments are more open-ended: actions in adaptive environments have unpredictable outcomes; in visionary environments, the market is malleable and there are no precedents; and shaping environments combine both sets of characteristics. Consequently, it is comparatively more difficult to learn the necessary approach to succeed in these environments. Finally, ambidexterity requires being able to cope effectively with all environments, introducing even more complexity.

As companies look to develop their talent, they need to take into account that some skills are harder to learn than others, and they should factor that into their overall talent strategy. For example, companies may seek to hire people with demonstrated skills and experience in difficult-to-learn environments like shaping, knowing that the required skills cannot be easily acquired. On the other hand, they might adopt a more organic approach for environments in which the required skills can be more easily learned, like classical.

Five Steps to Build Strategic Capabilities

As companies revamp their strategy and execution to match a variety of business environments, it is critical that they acquire, develop, and allocate the appropriate skill sets. In order to succeed, we propose a five-step approach for managing strategic talent.

1. *Diagnose your environment.* To determine which strategy approach to pursue, businesses need first to understand the nature of the environments in which they operate and compete. In particular, the unpredictability, malleability, and harshness of the environment have major implications for the appropriate approach to strategy – and the skills required to succeed. In a fast-changing business climate, however, leaders cannot rely on precedent, they must constantly monitor and diagnose whether the environments they face have changed.

   For example, Microsoft adjusted its approach to cloud computing along with changes in the environment. As Satya Nadella explained in his book about the company's transformation, early on the cloud market's evolution was unpredictable, so the company deployed an adaptive approach, making multiple bets on cloud capabilities – some of which succeeded, such as Azure, while others failed. As Microsoft gained more ground in the maturing cloud market through successful experiments, the company soon realized it could increasingly mold the market, and therefore adopted a shaping approach. This involved forming a wider ecosystem around its cloud products – including partnerships with competitors such as Google, Apple, and Linux – effectively utilizing the power of collaboration, as Nadella recognized when he said, "When done right, partnering grows the pie for everyone."[9]

2. *Deploy the right talent for different strategic challenges in different parts of the business.* Given the diversity of environments today, many organizations are facing different types of circumstances at once or over time. For example, a company's legacy business may require a classical approach, while its newest offerings may instead require, for instance, a shaping approach. Given the different strategy profiles that are required to succeed in different environments, companies should recruit, retain, and refocus their strategists according to the skills that are needed in each part of the business.

In order to do this effectively, organizations need first to assess and take stock of their talent pool. Only by having a view of the innate skills of its employees (by using games to assess their decision-making traits) can an organization then deploy employees effectively against different strategic challenges. Without having such a view of employees' innate skills, businesses risk putting their "strategists" in individually suboptimal situations, where they may not have the skills to execute the necessary approach.

An example of a company that employs this philosophy is Zappos, the online shoe and clothing retailer acquired for $1.2 billion by Amazon in 2009. A dedicated group in the organization develops a system of "badges"[10] that are awarded to employees based on their demonstrated skills. "What we're really trying to do and understand is what skills each and every individual has at the organization," said its lead organizational designer, John Bunch. The company developed a Role Marketplace in which employees looking for a project can apply to join teams looking for help – which in turn use the badges to identify the employees best fitted to the job. By effectively utilizing

9 Satya Nadella, Greg Shaw, and Jill Tracie Nichols, *Hit Refresh: The Quest to Rediscover Microsoft's Soul and Imagine a Better Future for Everyone*, HarperBusiness, 2017.
10 https://hbr.org/2016/07/beyond-the-holacracy-hype.

66 ——— Martin Reeves et al.

employees' skills across various projects, Zappos successfully adapted in a fast-changing market, achieving a 75% year-on-year increase in operating profits in the first year of implementing the model.

3. *Maintain a diversity of skills across the organization.* Our research showed that it is highly unlikely that an organization will have many ambidextrous leaders, who can succeed in any strategic environment. Therefore, to ensure success in heterogeneous strategic environments, companies need a balanced pool of individuals with different skill profiles.

Apple in the Steve Jobs era is a great example of embracing a diversity of skill profiles. For example, Tim Cook, then the COO, led classical parts of the business (such as supply chain management and manufacturing) by leveraging classical strategy skills – Cook described himself as "an engineer and an analytical person at heart." At the same time, Eddie Cue, then head of internet software and services – including products with uncertain business cases like iCloud and the App Store – was known for recognizing and persevering amid failures,[11] a necessary trait in adaptive environments: "We have to be honest with ourselves. We're not perfect, and we're going to make mistakes," Cue said. By having the right talent deployed in its various businesses, Apple was able to drive efficiency while constantly developing new growth engines.

4. *Broaden people's skills toward other environments.* Organizations need to develop an adequate talent pipeline to ensure a continuous supply of leaders who can succeed in different environments. With business environments rapidly changing – previous BCG research showed companies cycle through the growth-share matrix twice as fast on average as they did 20 years ago (see Chapter 4, "Revisiting the Growth-Share Matrix") – organizations need to continuously broaden their skill sets.

Our research showed that while the rates vary, strategy skills can indeed be learned, indicating that appropriate development programs could make a real impact, at least for some strategic environments. It is not common for companies to have career development programs that explicitly train future leaders to deploy several different strategy approaches. But ambidextrous leaders are increasingly valuable in diverse environments, so companies need to develop career paths across different environments, not just within one.

---

11 https://www.fastcompany.com/3062596/eddie-cue-and-craig-federighi-open-up-about-learning-from-apples-failures.

One way to achieve broad-based skill development is to institute a rotational program for managers, in which future leaders take on responsibilities in a variety of business units that require different strategic approaches. For example, Alibaba institutionalized regular changes at the level of business unit leadership. As former chief strategy officer Ming Zeng wrote, "The program not only helped further develop the skills of top talent, but also demonstrated throughout the entire organization the leadership's commitment to organizational flexibility."[12]

5. *Master data-driven skills testing and development.* To deploy the proposed talent strategy successfully, firms need objective measurements of individuals' talents and skills, including in relation to strategic challenges they may not have yet experienced. Taking a data and technology-driven approach to talent management has several advantages. First, it improves the company's ability to match people and situations, ensuring that the company has the right skills for success in each part of the business. Second, it increases the speed at which companies can match skills to strategic challenges. This is increasingly important today, as such changes occur with increasing frequency. Third, it provides a scalable assessment of the entire talent pool, allowing leaders to identify relevant talent from fringe areas of the company to address skill gaps. Fourth, the specific approach suggested here using strategy games and cognitive neuroscience measures is much more accurate than either subjective HR assessments or personality testing.

Since a one-size-fits-all approach to business strategy is no longer adequate in today's world, companies must also assess, develop, and deploy different skill sets to navigate different environments. A combination of neuroscience and strategy games is an accurate, scalable, rapid, and cost-effective way to achieve this.

---

12 Ming Zeng, *Smart Business: What Alibaba's Success Reveals About the Future of Strategy,* Harvard Business Review Press, 2018.

Part III: **Expanding the Boundaries of Strategy**

Ryoji Kimura, Martin Reeves, and Kevin Whitaker

Chapter 10
The New Logic of Competition

Many of today's business leaders came of age studying and experiencing a classical model of competition. Most large companies participated in well-defined industries selling similar sets of products; they gained advantage by pursuing economies of scale and capabilities such as efficiency and quality; and they followed a process of deliberate analysis, planning, and focused execution.

The traditional playbook for strategy is no longer sufficient. In all businesses, competition is becoming more complex and dynamic. Industry boundaries are blurring. Product and company lifespans are shrinking. Technological progress and disruption are rapidly transforming business. High economic, political, and competitive uncertainty is conspicuous and likely to persist for the foreseeable future.

Accordingly, in addition to the classical advantages of scale, companies are now contending with new dimensions of competition – *shaping* malleable situations, *adapting* to uncertain ones, and *surviving* harsh ones – which in turn require new approaches. And the stakes are higher than ever: the gap in performance between the top- and bottom-quartile companies has increased in each of the past six decades.[1]

Today's business leaders are dealing with complex competitive concerns in the short run. But they must also look beyond today's situation and understand at a more fundamental level what will separate the winners from the losers in the next decade. We see five new imperatives of competition that will come to the forefront for many businesses (Figure 10.1):

1. Increasing the rate of organizational learning
2. Leveraging multicompany ecosystems
3. Spanning both the physical and the digital world
4. Imagining and harnessing new ideas
5. Achieving resilience in the face of uncertainty

---

[1] Based on the average difference in EBIT margin between companies ranking in the top quartile and those in the bottom quartile in each of 71 industries (among US public companies with at least $50 million in revenue).

https://doi.org/10.1515/9783110755381-010

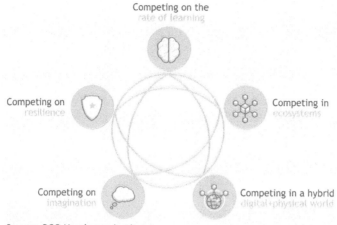

Source: BCG Henderson Institute.

Figure 10.1: The five new imperatives of competition.

In short, the logic of competition has changed from a predictable game with stable offerings and competitors to a complex, dynamic game that is played across many dimensions. Leaders who understand this, and re-equip their organizations accordingly, will be best positioned to win in the next decade.

Competing on the Rate of Learning

Learning has long been considered important in business. As Bruce Henderson, BCG's founder, observed more than 50 years ago,[2] companies can generally reduce their marginal production costs at a predictable rate as their cumulative experience grows. But in traditional models of learning, the knowledge that matters – learning how to make one product or execute one process more efficiently – is static and enduring. Going forward, it will instead be necessary to build organizational capabilities for dynamic learning – learning how to do new things, and "learning how to learn" by leveraging new technology.

Today, artificial intelligence, sensors, and digital platforms have already increased the opportunity for learning more effectively – but competing on the rate of learning[3] will become a necessity in the 2020s. The dynamic, uncertain

---

2 https://www.bcg.com/publications/1968/business-unit-strategy-growth-experience-curve.
3 https://www.bcg.com/publications/2018/competing-rate-learning.

business environment will require companies to focus more on discovery and adaptation rather than only on forecasting and planning.

Companies will therefore increasingly adopt and expand their use of AI, raising the competitive bar for learning. And the benefits will generate a "data flywheel" effect – companies that learn faster will have better offerings, attracting more customers and more data, further increasing their ability to learn.

For example, Netflix's algorithms take in behavioral data from the company's video streaming platform and automatically provide dynamic, personalized recommendations for each user. This improves the product, keeping more users on the platform for longer and generating more data to further fuel the learning cycle (Figure 10.2).

However, there is an enormous gap between the traditional challenge of learning to improve a static process and the new imperative to continuously learn new things throughout the organization. Therefore, successfully competing on learning will require more than simply plugging AI into today's processes and structures. Instead, companies will need to:

– Pursue a digital agenda that embraces all modes of technology relevant to learning – including sensors, platforms, algorithms, data, and automated decision making.
– Connect them in *integrated learning architectures* that can learn at the speed of data rather than being gated by slower hierarchical decision making.
– Develop business models that are able to create and act on dynamic, personalized customer insights.

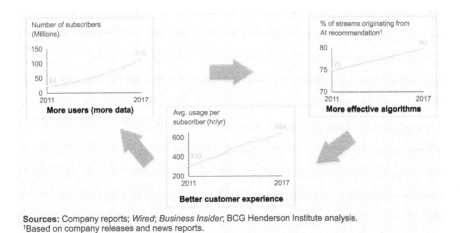

Sources: Company reports; *Wired*; *Business Insider*, BCG Henderson Institute analysis.
[1]Based on company releases and news reports.

Figure 10.2: Netflix's algorithms take in behavioral data from the company's video streaming platform and automatically provide dynamic, personalized recommendations for each user.

Competing in Ecosystems

Classical models of competition assume that discrete companies make similar products and compete within clearly delineated industries. But technology has dramatically reduced communication and transaction costs, weakening the Coasean logic for combining many activities inside a few vertically integrated firms.[4] At the same time, uncertainty and disruption require individual firms to be more adaptable, and they make business environments increasingly shapeable. Companies now have opportunities to influence the development of the market in their favor, but they can do this only by coordinating with other stakeholders.

As a result of these forces, new industrial architectures are emerging based on the coordination of *ecosystems* – complex, semifluid networks of companies that challenge several traditional business assumptions. Ecosystems blur the boundaries of the company. For example, platform businesses such as Uber and Lyft rely heavily on "gig economy" workers[5] who are not direct employees but rather temporary freelancers. Ecosystems also blur industry boundaries. For example, automotive ecosystems[6] include not just traditional suppliers but also connectivity, software, and cloud storage providers. And ecosystems blur the distinction between collaborators and competitors. For example, Amazon and third-party merchants have a symbiotic relationship, while the company competes with those merchants by selling private-label brands.

A few digital giants have demonstrated that successfully orchestrating ecosystems can yield outsized returns. Indeed, many of the largest and most profitable companies in the world are ecosystem-based businesses.[7] One example is Alibaba, which leads China's massive e-commerce market not by fulfilling most functions directly but by building platforms that connect manufacturers, logistics providers, marketers, and other relevant service providers with one another and with end users. By decentralizing business activities across large groups of firms or individuals, the Alibaba ecosystem is rapidly adaptive to consumers' needs and also highly scalable – resulting in 44% annualized revenue growth for the company in the past five years.

---

4 Ronald Coase, "The Nature of the Firm," 1937.

5 https://www.bcg.com/publications/2019/new-freelancers-tapping-talent-gig-economy.

6 https://www.bcg.com/publications/2019/emerging-art-ecosystem-management.

7 At the start of 2019, seven of the world's top ten companies by market capitalization leveraged multicompany ecosystems: Apple, Amazon, Microsoft, Alphabet, Facebook, Alibaba, and Tencent.

The playbook for how to emulate these ecosystem pioneers has not yet been fully codified, but a few imperatives are becoming increasingly clear:

- Adopt a fundamentally different perspective toward strategy, based on embracing principles like external orientation, common platforms, co-evolution, emergence, and indirect monetization.
- Determine what role your company can play in your ecosystem or ecosystems – not all companies can be the orchestrator.
- Ensure that your company creates value for the ecosystem broadly, not just for itself.

Competing in the Physical and the Digital World

Today's most valuable and fastest-growing businesses are disproportionately young technology companies, which operate ecosystems that are predominantly digital (Figure 10.3). But the low-hanging digital fruits in consumer services, including retail, information, and entertainment, seem to have been plucked. New opportunities are likely to come increasingly from digitizing the physical world, enabled by the rapid development and penetration of AI and the Internet of Things. This will increasingly bring tech companies into areas – such as B2B and businesses involving long-lived and specialized assets – that are still dominated by older incumbent firms.

DEMOGRAPHICS OF TOP TEN GLOBAL COMPANIES BY MARKET CAPITALIZATION

Primary sector[1]   Median company age[2]

Financials   Materials   Consumer Staples
Health Care   Energy   Technology

Sources: S&P Capital IQ; BCG Henderson Institute analysis.
Note: Based on market capitalization at beginning of year.
[1]Based on GICS classifications; Technology includes information technology, communications services, and internet services & retail.
[2]Years since company founding.

Figure 10.3: Today's most valuable and fastest-growing businesses are disproportionately young technology companies.

Early signs of "hybrid" competition at the physical-digital intersection[8] are already emerging. Digital giants are moving into physical sectors. For example, Amazon has opened new retail stores in addition to its acquisition of Whole Foods, while Google has entered automotive and transportation through its Waymo subsidiary. Meanwhile, incumbent companies are furiously pursuing digitization. For example, John Deere has invested heavily in IoT technology by adding connected sensors to its tractors and other equipment. The company collects and analyzes data from each machine, using the insights to provide updates to its equipment or suggestions to users. "Our roadmap is calling for machine learning and AI to find their way into every piece of John Deere equipment over time," said John Stone, the senior vice president for Deere's Intelligent Solutions Group.[9]

These trends point to a new battle between younger digital natives and traditional physical incumbents. But unlike in the past decade, where upstarts unseated many legacy leaders with purely digital models, the next round is likely to be a more balanced contest. Technology companies no longer have a limitless social license; in the next decade, they will have to navigate thorny issues like user trust, data privacy, and regulation, which will likely be even more critical in the context of hybrid competition. And incumbents will still have to fight against institutional inertia and the long odds of disruption,[10] but they will be able to better leverage existing relationships and expertise in the physical world. Therefore, the next wave of "natural selection" in business is likely to test *both* digital natives and incumbents – and winners could emerge from either group.

What will make the difference? To succeed in hybrid competition, companies will need to:

- Build strong relationships with actors on both sides of the ecosystem – customers *and* suppliers.
- Rethink existing business models in order to win the battle for new hybrid markets.
- Adopt good practices for governance of data and algorithms to preserve users' trust.

---

8 https://www.bcg.com/publications/2017/business-model-innovation-technology-digital-getting-physical-rise-hybrid-ecosystems.

9 Scott Ferguson, "John Deere Bets the Farm on AI, IoT," *Light Reading*, March 2018.

10 https://www.bcg.com/publications/2017/value-creation-strategy-transformation-creating-value-disruption-others-disappear.

Competing on Imagination

Companies can no longer expect to succeed by leaning predominantly on their existing business models. Long-run economic growth rates have declined in many economies, and demographics point to a continuation of that pattern. Competitive success has become less permanent over time.[11] And markets are increasingly shapeable, increasing the potential reward for innovation. As a result, the ability to generate new ideas is more important than ever.

However, creating new ideas is challenging for many companies. Inertia increases with age and scale, making it harder to create and harness new ideas: older and larger companies have less vitality[12] – the capacity for sustainable growth and reinvention (Figure 10.4). And business and managerial theory has emphasized a "mechanical" view, dominated by easily measurable variables like efficiency and financial outcomes, rather than focusing on how to create new ideas.

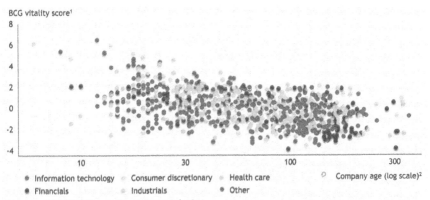

Source: BCG Henderson Institute analysis.
Note: Shows 1,083 companies worldwide (companies with $10 billion+ revenue or $20 billion+ market cap through year-end 2017; excludes energy, metals & mining, and commodity chemicals.
[1]Based on 18 metrics weighted by ability to predict future long-term growth; see "The Global Landscape of Corporate Vitality," BCG, 2018.
[2]Years since company founding.

Figure 10.4: Older and larger companies have less vitality – the capacity for sustainable growth and reinvention.

---

11 https://www.bcg.com/publications/2018/leaping-before-platform-burns-increasing-necessity-preemptive-innovation.
12 https://www.bcg.com/publications/2018/global-landscape-of-corporate-vitality.

To overcome these challenges, companies need to compete on imagination. Imagination lies upstream of innovation: to realize new possibilities, we first need inspiration (a reason to see things differently) and then imagination (the ability to identify possibilities that are not currently the case but could be). Imagination is a uniquely human capability – artificial intelligence today can make sense only of correlative patterns in existing data. As machines automate an increasing share of routine tasks, individual managers will need to focus on imagination to stay relevant and make an impact.

How can companies compete on imagination?

- Focus on anomalies, accidents, and analogies, rather than averages, in order to spark inspiration.
- Enable the open spread and competition of ideas – for example, by limiting hierarchy and empowering employees to experiment and make imaginative proposals.
- Become a "playful corporation" that is able to effortlessly explore new possibilities.

Competing on Resilience

Uncertainty is high on many fronts.[13] Technological change is disrupting businesses and bringing new social, political, and ecological questions to the forefront. Economic institutions are under threat from social divisions and political gridlock. Society is increasingly questioning the inclusivity of growth and the future of work. And planetary risks, such as climate change, are more salient than ever. Furthermore, deep-seated structural forces indicate this period of elevated uncertainty is likely to persist: technological progress will not abate; the rise of China as an economic power will continue to challenge international institutions; demographic trends point toward an era of lower global growth, which will further strain societies; and social polarization will continue to challenge governments' ability to effectively respond to national or global risks (Figure 10.5).

Under such conditions, it will become more difficult to rely on forecasts and plans. Business leaders will need to consider the larger picture, including economic, social, political, and ecological dimensions, making sure their companies can endure in the face of unanticipated shocks. In other words, businesses will effectively need to compete on resilience.

---

13 https://www.bcg.com/publications/2019/diagnosis-to-action-reflections-from-davos.

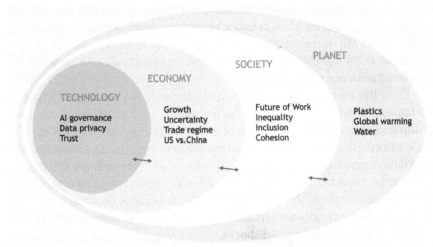

Source: BCG Henderson Institute.

Figure 10.5: Uncertainty is high on many fronts.

Survival is already challenging for many businesses today.[14] Building resilience is often at odds with traditional management goals like efficiency and short-run financial maximization. But to thrive sustainably in uncertain environments, companies must make resilience an explicit priority:

- Prepare for a range of scenarios to ensure that strategy is robust and risks are survivable.
- Build an adaptive organization that can rapidly adjust to new circumstances – for example, by constantly experimenting to identify new options.
- Proactively contribute to collective action on the biggest issues facing global economies and societies in order to maintain a social license to operate.

The New Significance of Scale

New forms of competition are highly intertwined. For example, companies that orchestrate ecosystems will have an advantage in competing on learning, because ecosystems are a rich source of real-time data and digital platforms

---

14 https://www.bcg.com/publications/2015/strategy-die-another-day-what-leaders-can-do-about-the-shrinking-life-expectancy-of-corporations.

facilitate experimentation. Many companies will integrate physical and digital assets by leveraging partnerships in hybrid ecosystems. Machine learning and autonomous action will increase humans' need for and ability to focus on imagination. And those shifts will collectively create further unpredictability for business, necessitating strategies for resilience.

These five emerging aspects of competition point to a new logic for "scale." No longer will scale represent only the traditional value of achieving cost leadership and optimizing the provision of a stable offering. Instead, new kinds of scale will create value across multiple dimensions: scale in the amount of relevant data companies can generate and access, scale in the quantity of learnings that can be extracted from this data, scale in experimentation to diversify the risks of failure, scale in the size and value of collaborative ecosystems, scale in the quantity of new ideas companies can generate, and scale in resilience to buffer the risks of unanticipated shocks.

Martin Reeves, Ryoji Kimura, Hiroaki Sugita, Saumeet Nanda, and James Yuji Grosvenor

Chapter 11
The Challenge of Slow

The coronavirus crisis has caused unprecedented disruption to businesses and economies around the world, forcing companies to respond on accelerated time-scales. Even prior to the pandemic, business environments around the world were changing faster than ever before, and outperformance was fading faster than it used to.[1] Business leaders are therefore understandably focused on in-creasing the agility of their organizations.

Yet while companies worry about fast and unforeseen changes, there are also many important *slow-moving* social, political, and ecological changes to navigate, too. These include the impact of climate change, increasing inequal-ity, the rise of China as an economic superpower, the development of Africa, and the growing importance of AI – all of which could have a significant impact on businesses in the long term. Even the COVID-19 outbreak presents a number of slower-moving challenges, such as shifts in attitudes and consumer behavior that will persist into the postcrisis future.[2]

In other words, companies need to think and operate on multiple time-scales[3] – both faster and slower. But navigating slow changes is not necessarily as easy as it might appear. Even when a slow phenomenon is well understood and highly predictable, as in the case of demographic change, it can nevertheless be challenging for companies to navigate. Why do companies falter in preparing for slow changes? What do the ones who successfully navigate slow change do differently? We looked into how companies responded to demographic change to find out more.

Demographic Aging: Slow Poison for Growth

Fertility rates are decreasing in almost all countries in the world. As a result, population growth has slowed, and some countries – including Germany, Italy,

---

1 https://sloanreview.mit.edu/article/fighting-the-gravity-of-average-performance/.

2 https://www.bcg.com/publications/2020/8-ways-companies-can-shape-reality-post-covid-19.

3 https://bcghendersoninstitute.com/fractal-strategy-2ce6898e9f13.

https://doi.org/10.1515/9783110755381-011

Japan, and Portugal – have already experienced population decline. Fertility decline, combined with increasing life expectancy, is leading to population aging.
The age distribution of the world population is moving from a pyramid shape to a
rectangle (Figure 11.1). While this trend is now visible worldwide, it started earlier
in wealthier countries, which are already experiencing its effects on economic
growth.

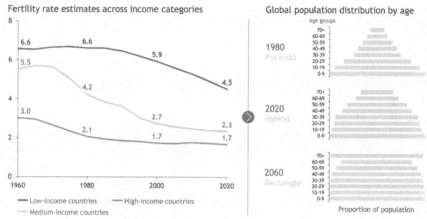

Sources: UN Department of Economic and Social Affairs, population division; BCG Henderson Institute
analysis.
Note: The categorization of income status is as per the United Nations.

Figure 11.1: The age distribution of the world population is moving from a pyramid shape to a
rectangle.

Economic growth in the long run is driven by two factors: growth in the labor
force and growth in labor productivity. Growth in the labor force contributed
about 30% of economic growth in the US from 1960 to 2010. However, retirement
of the post–World War II boomer generation and the subsequent decline in fertility rate have depressed labor force growth. The impact on economic growth is already visible. According to Oxford Economics, the 20-year average GDP growth
rate has already declined from above 3% before 2007 to 2.2% in 2018 and is
expected to stabilize around 1.75% to 2% during the next 20 years. The same
story is playing out at different speeds and with different time frames in all
major economies.

Economists forecast steady decline in world GDP growth from about 3.6%
in 2018 to 2.4% in the next 30 years (Figure 11.2). A long-term decline in economic growth will likely lead to a long-term decline in shareholder returns –
even though the past decade has, paradoxically, seen record-breaking market

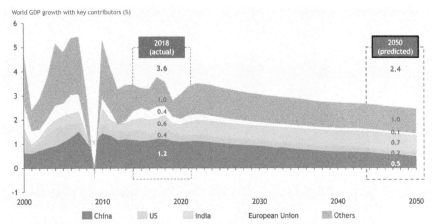

World GDP growth with key contributors (%)

Sources: Oxford Economics; BCG Henderson Institute analysis.
Note: Real GDP growth and projections were adjusted for purchasing-power parity. GDP predictions
as of 2019 do not take Coronavirus impact into account. Short-term GDP forecasts have been further
depressed ever since.

Figure 11.2: Economists forecast steady decline in world GDP growth.

returns. This disconnect between high market returns and depressed economic
growth in developed economies is driven by temporary factors, such as increased
debt and low interest rates fueling growth in P/E ratios, which cannot continue
forever. A demographically driven decline in GDP growth in major growth markets, such as China (which helped many companies compensate for sluggish domestic growth), and the rise of protectionism around the world will make this
kind of market outperformance less likely to occur in the future. However, investor expectations, which tend to be heavily influenced by past performance, may
continue to be high in the near to medium term, though they must eventually
decline. As a result, it is crucial for business leaders to find the right strategy for
growth in an impending lower-growth environment.

Japan: A Test Case for Adjusting to Population Aging

Fertility rate decline and societal aging started in Japan 10 to 20 years before other
developed economies and impacted both labor force and consumption; both have
been more or less stagnant for the past 20 years (Figure 11.3). This has contributed
to a sustained period of low economic growth and returns for Japanese companies.

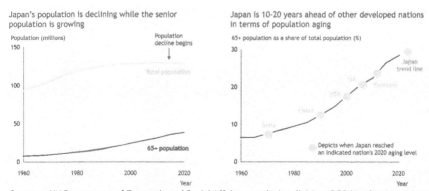

Japan's population is declining while the senior population is growing

Japan is 10-20 years ahead of other developed nations in terms of population aging

Sources: UN Department of Economic and Social Affairs, population division; BCG Henderson Institute analysis.

Figure 11.3: The Japanese labor force and consumption have been more or less stagnant for the past 20 years.

Japanese businesses and policymakers were well aware of the impending demographic pressures and their likely impact from early on. The 50-year population predictions made by the cabinet office of the Japanese government in 1999 have, so far, been more than 99% accurate. In 1996, in his very first press conference as prime minister, Ryutaro Hashimoto identified demographic change as the greatest threat to Japan's economy: ". . . from this demographic change alone, it is clear that we have to reform the system of the country. Otherwise, the reality is that the country will stop functioning."

The basic strategies for businesses to combat a demographics-led slowdown focus on two core issues: stagnation in consumption and a shortage of labor.

On the demand side, one option for Japanese corporations was to circumvent low domestic consumption by moving into higher-growth international markets. The other was to refocus on specific segments in the domestic market, which actually benefited from the demographic shift. Diaper, personal hygiene, and household cleaning products manufacturer Unicharm is a perfect example of a company that made both these strategies the cornerstone of its growth plan. In its 2001 annual report, the company announced that it had targeted two business opportunities: to develop its business in Asia and in the domestic adult incontinence sector.

Anticipating the growth slowdown in Japan, Unicharm started expanding into foreign markets as early as 1984, when it entered the Taiwanese market via a joint venture. After building presence in multiple Asian markets in the late 1980s and 1990s, the company dramatically accelerated its business expansion in Asia in the early 2000s and established itself as a market leader in its key product segments in such fast-growing markets as Thailand, Indonesia, and Vietnam. Foreign markets now contribute an impressive 60% of the company's revenues. This simple strategy has been adopted by other companies as well. Twelve out of the 14 Japanese large-cap companies that achieved annual shareholder returns of more than 10% for the period 1995 to 2018 earn more than 40% of their revenues from foreign markets. In contrast to these early movers, the majority of Japanese companies did not move aggressively to capture foreign markets, in spite of facing declining consumption growth in the 1990s. As late as 2002, only 13% of listed Japanese companies reported income from foreign countries – a number that almost tripled, to 38%, by 2018.

Even with aggregate stagnation in consumption, there were specific areas of domestic consumption growth. A good example is the diaper market in Japan. While adult diapers constitute only 15% of the total diaper market worldwide, they constitute more than 50% of the Japanese diaper market, driven by an aged population. Unicharm realized the potential of the incontinence market early and introduced its first diaper brand for adults in 1987. While customers with significant incontinence issues always required adult diapers, those with minor incontinence often avoided purchasing them due to lack of knowledge about products and social stigma associated with using them. With a differentiated product line that offered diapers designed for three different levels of incontinence, Unicharm actively expanded its market by educating customers. As of 2018, Unicharm was the market leader, with a share of more than 50% in the adult diaper market. Procter & Gamble, the global leader in the total diaper market, did not focus on this high-growth segment and failed to capture significant share. As a result, P&G exited the Japanese adult incontinence market in 2007.

On the supply side, utilizing readily available and lower-cost labor in foreign countries became a much-discussed potential strategy in the 1980s to combat high local wages and tight labor markets. While many Japanese manufacturers started establishing production facilities in low-cost economies, they were very cautious in moving significant amount of production overseas. By 1992, when General Motors had moved 40%, and IBM had moved 46%, of production outside the US, only 20% of Toyota's and 8% of Hitachi's production had moved offshore. Even as late as 2005, when 63% of Japanese manufacturers had foreign production facilities, only 20% of the production in these companies was performed offshore. This has contributed to 2.5 million unfilled job openings in Japan, a number that is growing by 6% per year.

Population aging leads not only to labor shortages but also to changes in the age mix of the labor force. As previously noted, the global population structure is moving from a pyramid shape to a rectangle (Figure 11.4). However, hierarchical organizational structures largely remain pyramid shaped, creating a

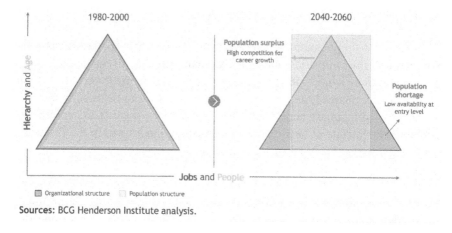

Sources: BCG Henderson Institute analysis.

Figure 11.4: Hierarchical organizational structures largely remain pyramid shaped, creating a shortage of young workers for entry-level jobs and a surplus of older workers.

shortage of young workers for entry-level jobs and a surplus of older workers. This leads to high competition for young talent and limited prospects for getting senior managerial roles. Although few companies have seriously tried to tackle this challenge, some success stories include such companies as retail giant AEON and furniture retailer Nitori, which try to make nonmanagerial jobs more feasible for older workers by using tools to simplify physically strenuous work and providing special facilities, such as resting places. Other companies are moving away from traditional rigid and hierarchical organizational structures to allow for more flexible career paths. For instance, SB Technology has introduced grade skips, and software company Line has opted to compensate its engineers with differential salaries based on technical expertise. However, such examples are rare among a sea of companies that have not changed their organizational setups significantly.

Why do Companies Fail to Adapt to Slow Changes?

This brings us to the core question: why do the majority of companies fail to adapt to slow changes? Three types of organizational failures weaken a company's ability to deal with slow changes.

1. *Failure to* see. When evaluating future choices, we use discount rates to adjust future outcomes to present value, so that they can be compared and strategic choices can be made. In certain contexts, individuals and organizations tend to apply *hyperbolic discounting*. This is a phenomenon where discount rates increase with longer timescales. Because the present is clear, while the future is often hazy, there is a bias toward maximizing the present at the cost of the future. Slow-moving changes can have a significant long-term impact, but future scenarios may be hard to predict or imagine. This pushes many business leaders to focus on optimizing current business models rather than imagining new ones. In 2007, for instance, P&G saw adult incontinence as a niche market, significant only in the unique market structure in Japan. Hence, the company sold its Japanese adult diaper brand to concentrate on products with more global appeal. But P&G failed to visualize the potential of the adult incontinence market not only in Japan but also in the rapidly aging economies of Europe and North America, and it had to change course some years later. In 2014, the company launched a new adult diaper brand in order to avoid losing out on the growing market in the US.

   Slow changes can give rise to a perception that there is plenty of time to deal with them. However, this *illusion of time* can prove dangerous because dealing with slow changes may require immediately embarking on long-term investments. For instance, establishing yourself in a foreign market is an expensive and time-consuming strategy. Many companies in Japan delayed the process of expanding abroad during a high-growth period in the 1970s and 1980s. As a result, after the slump of the late 1980s, they were too busy firefighting in their domestic markets to seize overseas opportunities.

   It is important to note that our Japan example deals with the unusual situation of *very predictable* long-term change. The challenges discussed here are further exacerbated with phenomena that are much less predictable, such as the rise of service robots and the impact of climate change. Uncertainty creates further barriers to imagining and preparing for the future.

2. *Failure to* care. Another key factor that contributes to hyperbolic discounting is the *incentive structure* for business leaders, which is primarily focused on achieving success on a timescale of one to five years because of both market pressures and career promotion cycles. Slow changes, by their nature, have minimal impact on short timescales. Hence, they have a high tendency to get overlooked, especially if the strategy to deal with them involves significant investments that don't reap immediate rewards or penalties for leaders but will impact their successors. Many companies have scenario-planning exercises, but it's hard to act against a future possibility if it involves siphoning

funds from a sure-bet current business, especially in a company that is run on short-term financial metrics.

3. *Failure to* act. There is a tendency of mature and successful organizations to continue on their current trajectory due to *organizational inertia*. MIT Sloan professor Donald Sull states that organizational inertia stems from a company's inability to change its routines, relationships, values and, most important, *strategic frame* – the set of assumptions that determine how managers view and think about their businesses.

   The failure of Japanese companies to move sufficient production offshore despite opening foreign factories can be ascribed to such organizational inertia. Relationships and processes established with domestic vendors, as well as relationships with employees and local communities, stopped companies from downsizing Japanese factories, in spite of the writing on the wall. False beliefs, such as assuming that precision or quality manufacturing is impossible in foreign countries, only reinforced this inertia.

   In extreme cases, companies end up actively reinforcing narratives that rationalize sticking to the status quo. This phenomenon is exacerbated by the *ostrich effect* – a bias against receiving or acknowledging information that can point to a contrary view of the future.

How to Avoid Such Failures

Companies can take five actions to make sure they respond adequately to slow-moving change.

1. *Visualize.* Clear visualization of the future and quantitative exploration of options help dispel hyperbolic discounting.[4] (See "An Illustration of the Power of Visualization.") When clear forecasting of the future is not possible, *scenario analysis* is a very useful tool for examining multiple plausible futures and their consequences.

---

4 Eran Magen, Carol S. Dweck, and James J. Gross, "The Hidden Zero Effect: Representing a Single Choice as an Extended Sequence Reduces Impulsive choice," *Psychological Science*, 2008 Jul; 19(7): 648–649.

An Illustration of the Power of Visualization

A classic experiment in hyperbolic discounting asked participants to choose between receiving $50 today or $70 in a year. Scientists then ran another experiment with a more explicit articulation of the same choices: $50 today and $0 in a year or $0 today and $70 in a year. A significantly higher number of participants chose the delayed reward with the more explicit articulation. The fewest participants opted for the delayed options when they were asked to choose between $50 today or $70 at some unspecified later time.

It is important to visualize not only the future environment but also the potential response of competitors. Unicharm's analysis rightly identified the impending growth slowdown in Japan and the consumption boom in other Asian markets. But the company also anticipated competition from global fast-moving consumer goods giants, which would eventually act on similar analyses. Assuming that these companies would focus on the largest markets, such as China and India, Unicharm decided initially to invest heavily in relatively smaller high-growth markets, such as Indonesia, Thailand, and Vietnam in order to attain market leadership.

2. *Align incentives.* Central to the success of any long-term strategy is leadership's vision and commitment. Hence, it is critical for company leaders to have a stake in its long-term future. Takahisa Takahara, the son of Unicharm founder Keiichiro Takahara, joined the company in 1991 and held various management positions before becoming its president in 2001 – a position that he still occupies today. His long history in the company and extended leadership tenure supported his visionary leadership style and allowed him to focus on finding the next source of long-term growth.

   This long-term perspective is reinforced by the fact that Unicharm is a family company, albeit a public one. Our research shows that family companies tend to take a more prudent and long-term view, presumably because, for them, the force of market pressures is balanced by long-term incentives.

3. *Create urgency.* Slow changes are often treated as nonurgent, which exacerbates organizational inertia. Creating a sense of urgency is, therefore, a necessary antidote. In 1999, Jeff Bezos, the founder and CEO of Amazon, pulled 300 of the company's employees into a room and announced that Amazon was dying. This was a surprise to the employees, who had just seen their company produce spectacular growth. Bezos had identified the digitization of goods and services as a slow change that would have a massive impact on the business in the coming decades, because he believed that books, music, and videos – the three major contributors to Amazon's sales at the time – would be easily digitizable. Bezos created a sense of urgency to both digitize and rapidly diversify into other product categories. In the three core

categories, Amazon became the disruptor itself, with the introduction a decade later of the Kindle ecosystem, Amazon prime music, and Amazon Prime Video. Diversification decreased the risk of this transition.

In addition to scenario planning, urgency toward slow changes can be triggered by two other sources: threat of action from competitors and shifting demands from customers. Unicharm's urgent need to enter the markets in Indonesia, Thailand, and Vietnam was driven by the fear of losing out to global giants, such as Procter & Gamble. The company's focus on expanding in the adult incontinency market was driven by declining domestic demand for their baby and childcare products.

Exercises can be constructed[5] to exploit these two sources of fear and to drive companies to take timely actions. A *maverick scan* involves evaluating the investments being made by venture funds and disruptors in your markets or in adjacent ones. In the exercise, you need to understand the essence of the bets made by these mavericks against your business model and the consequences for you if these bets are correct. This helps you understand the conditions for these bets to work and your best strategy in this scenario. While most maverick strategies are risky, an improved ability to predict when they can work helps you self-disrupt or build your defenses in a timely manner.

Another useful exercise is to *understand customers in emerging niches* who are not direct targets of your core offering. The purpose of this exercise is to form a strategy for a scenario in which this customer segment is the only one that you have to cater to. For instance, adult diapers were seen as a niche health care product catering to customers with severe incontinence issues. However, by understanding customers with minor incontinence issues, Unicharm was able to imagine, build, and dominate a new, attractive market segment. New signals from new, potential, or existing customers can help drive up urgency within an organization a lot more effectively than internal change advocates can.

4. *Commit resources.* Slow-moving changes are often well known. Most companies today have a climate action group. Most leadership teams are aware of growing markets for the elderly, the rise of AI, and greater health consciousness in society. Still, only a small proportion of companies have gone beyond token actions against these trends. A key reason underlying why many Japanese companies could not do what Unicharm did was their discomfort in shifting resources away from existing, successful businesses.

---

5 https://bcghendersoninstitute.com/free-up-your-mind-to-free-up-your-strategy-4bec09783291.

After declaring their intention to move into Asian markets, Unicharm was ready to dedicate the resources required to succeed. The company moved some of its top executives to lead foreign businesses. The head of sales, one of the top five leaders of the company, became the head of Chinese business, and the deputy head of sales led the Indonesian business. Unicharm invested heavily to acquire local companies to build a sales network and market share in new markets. The R&D resources of the company were focused on building low-cost products customized for each new foreign market. The manufacturing footprint was shifted to low-cost economies, and the supply chain headquarters was moved from Tokyo to Shanghai in order to support Asian markets. It is important to note that all of these investments came at the cost of reduced resource allocation to the Japanese market, which still contributed more than 85% of the company's revenues in 2000. Since then, Unicharm has seen about 9% year-over-year revenue growth, with almost 75% of the growth contributed by foreign markets – which, in total, now account for 60% of Unicharm's revenues.

5. *Develop action bias.* Companies that focus on heavily exploiting existing competitive advantages find it hard to change themselves. Companies that are biased toward experimentation and exploring new options tend to suffer less organizational inertia. The real reason why Amazon could respond to Jeff Bezos's call for urgency is because the organization is perpetually in motion – a trait that Bezos has famously popularized as the "Day 1 mindset." Whether through incremental changes (adding new product categories and automating warehouses, for example) or quantum leaps (adding new verticals, such as AWS and Kindle), the company is always changing – and thus has never fallen into the comfort zone of a fixed routine. As Bezos has said, "Day 2 is stasis. Followed by irrelevance. Followed by excruciating, painful decline. Followed by death. And *that* is why it is *always* Day 1." Such vitality[6] in companies is essential to deal with fast changes. It also improves their ability to implement strategy to combat slow changes.

In a rapidly changing, technology-fueled world, leaders need to become attuned to a faster pace of change. But they must also attend to the significant challenges and opportunities presented by slower change. They need to become multi-clock-speed organizations.

---

6 https://bcghendersoninstitute.com/in-search-of-vital-companies-560b7450ba98.

Chapter 12
Strategy on Multiple Timescales

Businesses and societies today increasingly face the challenge of strategizing across multiple timescales. As artificial intelligence makes it possible to act in seconds or milliseconds, and social and environmental issues that develop over decades become more pressing, the relevant timescales are being expanded in both directions – faster and slower – making the challenge of managing trade-offs across timescales more critical.

The traditional toolkit does not seem to be up to this challenge. Businesses have traditionally considered a narrow set of issues that operate at a consistent clock speed; but an expanding range of relevant timescales and the increased expectation that businesses will behave in a socially responsible manner mean that these simplifications are no longer appropriate. New approaches are needed.

Many phenomena across a wide range of fields exhibit the general problem of making trade-offs or balancing action on different timescales. These diverse phenomena and the solutions that have been developed against them can help to achieve a better understanding of the nature of the problem and potential elements of a more successful approach.

By synthesizing insights across different fields and perspectives, we identify two fundamental issues that need to be addressed by a multi-timescale strategy, and a common set of principles upon which solutions can be developed:

1. *Different timescales are often intertwined.* What happens on one timescale affects what can be done on other timescales. Furthermore, long-term phenomena are often highly uncertain. As a result, multi-timescale problems generally cannot be separated into a set of single-timescale problems and solved independently. Emerging strategies that can address multi-timescale problems holistically include:
   - Embrace contradiction.
   - Leverage simple rules for "good enough" outcomes.
   - Design decision architectures that promote a balanced focus on different scales.
   - Map and understand the dynamics of the larger systems within which you operate.
   - Use adaptive strategies.
   - Make decisions with progressive commitment.

https://doi.org/10.1515/9783110755381-012

2. *Long-term problems are generally collective problems.* Many of the challenges on longer timescales that businesses face, such as maintaining sustainability of the environmental or economic context, cannot be sufficiently addressed by individual organizations alone. Instead, cooperation and collaboration are required. Emerging strategies that can address this issue include:
   - Don't treat the "prisoners' dilemma" as inevitable – collective action problems can become coordination games instead.
   - Create better metrics of progress toward long-term goals.
   - Leverage financial markets to illuminate and amplify existing beliefs.
   - Articulate compelling goals and narratives.
   - Pursue bottom-up approaches.

Why Strategizing on Multiple Timescales is Increasingly Critical

Environmental and social trends are stretching societies and creating new challenges. For example, cities have traditionally been designed for immediate convenience and amenities, but climate change and its effects have brought additional considerations into play, such as managing future flood risk. Many high-risk areas are starting to reconsider their approach to development to address these risks.[1] But perceptions about risks and solutions differ, and whereas the benefits of mitigation will generally not be realized for decades, its costs are realized today – so action has varied widely across cities. Similarly, recent power outages driven by extreme weather events have sparked a discussion about whether and how to invest in weather-proofing electricity grids in Texas and elsewhere, albeit at a cost in the present.

Many businesses are also grappling with the challenge of figuratively "weather-proofing" their organizations against future risks. COVID-19 has highlighted the impact of unpredictable shocks, as well as the long-term value of business resilience. And companies are increasingly committing to take action on pressing societal issues such as decarbonization. But such actions similarly have uncertain future benefits and the potential to contradict near-term goals.

These problems are all examples of a common challenge: how to strategize across multiple timescales. Businesses and societies generally must deal with

---

1 "Waterfront designers rise to the challenge of flood risk," *Financial Times*, 2021.

phenomena that operate on different timescales (from the near term to the long term), often involving trade-offs. Actions that address one timescale may undercut effective action on another (for example, development in a fragile area may be desired in the short run but may increase the potential long-term damage of floods). Systems optimized for one timescale may not be effective for another (for example, a company designed to maximize efficiency in the short run may be less resilient to long-term risks). And resources spent against one phenomenon cannot be used against another (for example, investing in decarbonization may reduce a business's capacity to invest in developing its next product).

Businesses and societies have always had to manage across multiple timescales, but the challenge has become much more important and complex today. Whereas social and environmental issues that operate over decades could once be treated as constants in the short run for later consideration, many such shifts (such as climate change, rising inequality within many nations, and falling biodiversity) have progressed to the point where they are becoming relevant in the present. And whereas very short timescales of seconds and milliseconds could once be considered irrelevant, the increased speed and reach of artificial intelligence and digital platforms have brought these into focus.

Business strategy has traditionally considered a narrow set of issues (such as customer needs, operating model effectiveness, and competitive advantage), a limited range of timescales (most notably the annual planning process) and a limited number of stakeholders (customers, employees, competitors). Such simplification may have made sense when contextual change was slow, and when the only expectation of businesses was that they would aim to maximize their own financial performance. But with technological and contextual change accelerating, and with a greater expectation that businesses behave in a socially responsible manner, leaders need to expand the range of timescales and stakeholders they consider – which will require new approaches to managing trade-offs between them.

Seeking Inspiration from a Range of Perspectives

Managing across multiple timescales is a general challenge that can be found in many fields: though the details vary, a number of phenomena demonstrate the problem of making trade-offs or balancing action on different timescales. By seeing the challenge through these different perspectives and synthesizing them, we can better understand the nature of the problem and identify some common solution elements.

To explore these different perspectives, we assembled a dozen minds from different fields in science and business for a wide-ranging discussion of multi-timescale problems.

- Perspectives from evolutionary and systems science were shared by Stephanie Forrest, Professor of Computer Science at Arizona State University and director of the Biodesign Center for Biocomputation, Security and Society; and Simon Levin, the James S. McDonnell Distinguished University Professor and Director of the Center for BioComplexity at Princeton University.
- Perspectives from psychology and economics were shared by Peter Turchin, an evolutionary anthropologist at the Complexity Science Hub Vienna and the University of Connecticut; and Elke Weber, the Gerhard R. Andlinger Professor in Energy and the Environment and Professor of Psychology and Public Affairs at Princeton University and founder and director of the Behavioral Science for Policy Lab.
- Perspectives from capital markets and economics were shared by Philipp Carlsson-Szlezak, BCG's Chief Economist and a Managing Director and Partner in the firm's New York office; Anne Maria Eikeset, an ecologist and evolutionary biologist and a researcher at Norges Bank Investment Management with a particular focus on climate and environmental change and their impact on investments; Peter Hancock, the former President and CEO of AIG; and Nick Silitch, Chief Risk Officer of Prudential Financial.
- Perspectives from business and innovation were shared by Maria Hancock, an angel investor who has two decades of experience in technology, risk management and asset management; and Martin Reeves, Chairman of the BCG Henderson Institute and a Senior Partner and Managing Director in BCG's San Francisco office.
- Perspectives from sustainability were shared by Georg Kell, Chairman of the Board of Arabesque (a technology company that uses AI and big data to assess sustainability performance relevant for investment analysis and decision making) and the founding Director of the United Nations Global Compact; and David Young, a Senior Partner and Managing Director in the Boston Office of BCG and a Fellow of the BCG Henderson Institute studying the role of the corporation in society and sustainable business model innovation.

This chapter presents a summary of key multi-timescale phenomena and solution ideas from these specific fields and concludes with a synthesis of insights that we hope can provide inspiration for leaders to develop strategies to meet this challenge.

Five Perspectives on Multi-Timescale Strategies

Phenomena and Solution Ideas from Evolutionary and Systems Science

Multi-timescale phenomena: One type of multi-timescale problem is observed in cancer management. Treatments that kill tumor cells, such as aggressive chemotherapy, can be effective in the short run. However, in the longer term, such treatments may shorten the period over which the drug is likely to be effective by applying selection pressure across the different genotypes comprising a tumor and selecting for those that are resistant to treatment. Analogous problems can be found in pest management, where pesticides can reduce infestation in the short run but select for resistant types over time,[2] or in the use of antibiotics to treat human or animal diseases.

Trade-offs between timescales must also be made in cybersecurity. If the reaction against a short-term threat is too strong, it risks accelerating the arms race with cyber-attackers, bringing forward new threats.

Evolution poses another type of multi-timescale problem: the trade-off involved in *maintaining capabilities* when they are not needed immediately. Sometimes, genetic lines lose traits that are not useful (for example, many insect species on secluded islands have lost the ability to fly).[3] But many traits are maintained even when they are not immediately useful, sometimes for long-term benefit. For example, aspen trees in Yellowstone National Park typically use vegetative reproduction; but after major forest fires created new conditions that could only be reforested via seeds, aspen trees made surprisingly rapid recoveries, demonstrating that they had retained germination capabilities.

Solutions: Treatment regimes have been developed that address multiple timescales simultaneously. For example, adaptive cancer therapy does not aim to eliminate a tumor, but instead aims to merely keep it from growing and metastasizing, reducing the risk of unwanted selection pressure for resistant cells.[4] Similarly, adaptive pest management and antibiotic therapy aim to balance the short-term benefits to individuals against the long-term risks of resistance to individuals and societies.

In evolution, organisms often adopt a strategy of progressive irreversibility – when a change to the environment is detected, organisms will take reversible

---

2 https://link.springer.com/article/10.1007/s13593-015-0327-9.
3 Harrison, R. G., "Dispersal polymorphism in insects," *Annual Review of Ecological Systematics*, 11, pp. 95–118, 1980.
4 https://www.nature.com/articles/s41467-017-01968-5.

actions first (such as shivering in response to the cold), and only later moving to progressively more irreversible actions (such as ultimately evolving over generations to become inherently better-suited for cold weather).[5] This preserves optionality, reducing the likelihood of getting locked into a suboptimal path for a transient benefit (Figure 12.1).

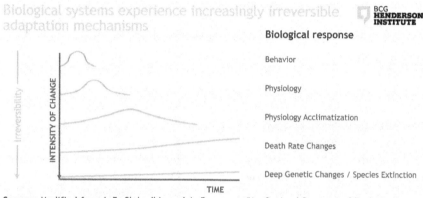

Source: Modified from L.B .Slobodkin and A. Rapoport, "An Optimal Strategy of Evolution", Quart, *Review of Biology*, Vol. 49, No. 3 (1974), pp. 181-200

Figure 12.1: In evolution, organisms often adopt a strategy of progressive irreversibility.

Another important insight from biology is that many phenomena that operate on longer timescales also operate on larger spatial scales: for instance, in the study of ecology, the length of timescale on which a phenomenon operates tends to be correlated with the level of aggregation involved.[6]

Insights from Psychology and Anthropology

Multi-timescale problems: When deciding whether and how to prepare for catastrophic risks individuals must balance the cost of preparation, which generally accrues in the short term, with the benefit of avoiding catastrophe, which will only later become evident. As demonstrated by many institutions'

5 Slobodkin, L. B. and Rapoport, A., "An optimal strategy of evolution," *Quarterly Review of Biology*, 49, pp. 181–200, 1974.
6 https://www.researchgate.net/figure/Stommel-diagram-showing-time-and-space-scales-for-typical-biophysical-phenomenon_fig3_305418677.

unpreparedness for the COVID-19 crisis, longer-term threats are often ignored until they impinge on the present.[7]

Furthermore, managing such problems is complicated by the *"bounded rationality"* of human decision-making: finite attention and processing capacity mean that it is often not feasible to optimize over all timescales simultaneously.[8] As a result, individuals often default to dealing with only one goal at a time to simplify the challenge, which can lead to a bias toward immediate concerns.

At a larger scale, society-wide behavior must also be understood on multiple timescales. For example, social instability is driven by feedback loops on several timescales: macro-scale processes such as demographic trends play out over centuries; meso-scale processes such as intrastate conflict play out over decades; and micro-scale processes such as individual acts of violence play out over hours or days. Leaders aiming to maintain stability must consider all timescales. However, these feedback loops interact in non-intuitive ways, and may have very delayed effects, making it difficult to understand the system and identify useful interventions.

Solutions: To overcome challenges of bounded rationality, individuals apply a range of heuristics to make decisions faster and with less complexity. Though such heuristics occasionally lead to sub-optimal outcomes, they generally provide "good-enough" results in most circumstances and overcome the limitations on human information processing capacity and appetite.

Another remedy is to design *"choice architectures"* to promote a balanced focus across timescales. One way of achieving this is with automaticity: for example, if an investor is prone to overreact to short-term phenomena at the expense of focusing on longer term issues, they may implement automatic rebalancing rules into their portfolios to avoid the need for frequent manual adjustments. Another mechanism involves incentives: different metrics or rewards can encourage attention toward longer timescales, countering natural myopic tendencies.

At organizational or societal scales, it is also possible to leverage *delegation* and *comparative advantage* to ensure challenges on each timescale receive sufficient focus in total. For example, governments generally delegate the short-term task of policing compliance with existing laws to one public body and the longer-term task of making or updating laws for the future to another. Similarly, different investors can complement each other by focusing on different timescales.

---

7 https://www.foreignaffairs.com/articles/2020-10-13/heads-sand.
8 Simon, H. A., *Models of man; social and rational.* Wiley, 1957.

Finally, leaders can *improve their understanding of the structure and dynamics of the larger system* to identify policies or interventions that will lead to positive outcomes. By understanding how responses to interventions or natural experiments unfold, feedback loops and time constants can be understood, creating a foundation for multi-timescale strategy.

Insights from Capital Markets and Economics

Multi-timescale problems: Economic policy decisions often involve trade-offs among different timescales, because what is helpful in the short term is not always sustainable in the long run. Public debt may be used to fund programs that are beneficial in the short run, but in the long run it can make future borrowing more expensive or even cause broader financial system issues (though opinions vary widely on when that point arrives). Entitlement spending programs can improve living standards in the short run, but some may become unsustainable in the long run. And loosening of bank capital requirements may increase credit and short-run economic activity, especially during certain crises, but may also increase systemic risks in the long run.

For investors, the challenge of pricing financial assets itself often requires thinking on multiple timescales, because many assets are valued based on future expectations. An investor deciding what price to pay for equity must consider not only the company's short-term profit potential but its long-term value, which will necessarily be affected by slow contextual change and risk factors. On the flip side, an investor may choose to participate in an asset bubble if they believe prices will still rise in the short run, even if an eventual deflation is inevitable.

A further complication is that *market participants may have very different time horizons*. For example, active asset managers often must achieve short-term outperformance or else face withdrawal of funds, whereas pension funds and life insurers adopt a longer-term focus. Even within an institution, time horizons may vary.

Finally, the *price signals* that financial markets provide to policymakers and other actors must be interpreted on different timescales as well. For example, through the early 20th century, the pound sterling was considered the global "reserve currency," giving the country a greater ability to borrow for short-term spending; but unsustainable borrowing slowly erodes reserve currency status, as eventually occurred when sterling was replaced by the US dollar.

Solutions: A common adage in policymaking is that leaders must "first win to govern" – long-term goals can only be pursued if short-term promises are made to win election – effectively taking one timescale as a constraint on which the other can be optimized. The opposite philosophy might be an investing mantra of "never bet the full bankroll" – short-term winnings should be maximized only after satisfying the long-term goal of survival.

Investors facing a contradiction in timescales may be able to resolve the contradiction through persuasion: a sufficiently credible investor expecting a bubble to burst may be able to convince other market participants of that thesis, precipitating an orderly and timely exit.

And because they create valuable information, *financial market mechanisms* themselves can be seen as a solution to the problem of quantifying long-term risks. For example, to help calibrate the trade-off between the short-term benefits of economic stimulus and the longer-run risk of heightened inflation, policymakers can infer aggregate inflation expectations from the spread between nominal bond yields and inflation-protected yields. Such transparency about consensus beliefs can not only improve individual actors' ability to manage trade-offs across timescales, it can also facilitate collective action against long-term issues. For example, experiments have shown that cooperation is more likely when there is agreement about the amount of progress that needs to be made.[9]

Insights from Business and Innovation

Multi-timescale problems: A company must manage many trade-offs that operate across timescales. One such notable trade-off is the balance between exploiting its current business and exploring new potential businesses: devoting more resources to marketing the existing product will generally maximize short-term returns, but to survive in the long run a company also needs to create new offerings or business models.[10]

Another such challenge is the trade-off between short-term financial maximization and system-wide sustainability. Many actions of profit-maximizing businesses can have negative long-term effects on the environmental and social systems in which they are embedded – and if those systems collapse, businesses will also not survive in the long run.

Although aggregate business and economic growth has been driven by continuous technological progress, creating and harnessing new innovations requires efforts taken on multiple timescales. These include basic research with a

---

9 Barrett and Dannenberg, "Climate negotiations under scientific uncertainty," *Proceedings of the National Academy of Sciences*, 2012.

10 Haanaes, K., Reeves, M., and Wurlod, J., "The Two Percent Company," *BCG.com*, 2018.

long time horizon to identify new technologies; entrepreneurship with a moderate time horizon to turn them into products; and scaling in large organizations with shorter time horizons to make them more widely accessible; all of which must be harnessed and balanced to create a thriving innovation ecosystem.

To make trade-offs over time, business leaders have traditionally been trained to model different potential outcomes across timescales, weight them with a discount rate, and select the approach with the highest expected value. But for many emerging challenges, these tools are insufficient.

For one thing, many long-term phenomena often cannot be precisely quantified. For instance, when calibrating the trade-off of reducing short-term efficiency for the long-term benefit of building resilience, calculating the short-term cost is usually trivial, but calculating the long-term benefit requires a projection of the likelihood and expected impact of future shocks – which are not perfectly knowable because the number of plausible scenarios is high, probability distributions could change, and developments may be path-dependent.[11]

For another, organizations and individuals are often susceptible to hyperbolic discounting – applying a discount rate that varies over time (higher in the short term and lower in the long term), which leads to inconsistent trade-offs. Hyperbolic discounting arises naturally when different exponential discount curves are combined and averaged, making it a natural outcome in organizations or societies composed of individuals with different discount rates.

Finally, optimizing for the expected utility is often insufficient: strict utility maximization can lead to the selection of strategies with an expected value that grows exponentially but a chance of catastrophic failure that approaches certainty in the long run (as in Gambler's Ruin).[12] Such an outcome is not favorable for businesses, which need longevity as well as expected value.

Solutions: To address the challenge of making trade-offs among timescales, leaders have developed some simple heuristics to rebalance their efforts. One such example is the "balanced scorecard," which dictates that all relevant timescales must be addressed to at least some extent.

Some businesses have also improved their ability to calibrate trade-offs across timescales by adopting new, forward-looking metrics.[13] For example, measuring a company's "vitality" (its capacity for sustainable future growth) can shed light on

---

11 Reeves, M., Levin, S., et al., "Resilience vs. Efficiency: Calibrating the Tradeoff," *BCG Henderson Institute*, 2020.

12 Lewontin, R. and Cohen, D., "On population growth in a randomly varying environment," *Proceedings of the National Academy of Sciences*, 62, pp. 1056–1060, 1969.

13 https://www.thorntontomasetti.com/resource/2019-annual-report-vitality.

how well the company is positioned to succeed on longer timescales, providing signals about whether or how to rebalance trade-offs.

Companies can also be designed to make short-term failures less catastrophic, increasing resilience on longer timescales. For example, modularization (which many digital platforms employ today) allows for the easy replacement of capabilities: if one provider fails or becomes obsolete, a new provider can easily take their place. Businesses designed for modularity can reduce the likelihood of fatal short-term shocks and also adapt to long-term changes more easily.[14]

Finally, many leaders are articulating a new role for corporations, replacing the single objective of maximizing short-run financial returns with a balanced goal of thriving on multiple timescales by serving multiple stakeholders.

Insights from Sustainability

Multi-timescale problems: The most pressing challenges in sustainability fundamentally involve trade-offs across multiple timescales: the benefits of mitigation play out over very long timescales, while the costs of such actions are incurred in the present day. This applies to a wide range of sustainability issues, such as *climate change, species depletion, chemical pollution,* and *disaster preparedness.*

For governments, NGOs, and public bodies, the challenge is balancing the trade-off over time – calibrating the short-term costs and long-term benefits as well as aligning beliefs about them to promote effective action. For other actors like businesses and investors, the problem is less direct but still present – sustainable natural and social systems are necessary to preserve business and financial systems in the long term.

However, different actors face different incentives: politicians may be most concerned about what happens before the next election, whereas the public at large may have a much longer-term horizon. The potential costs are often borne by different stakeholders than the potential benefits, further complicating the challenge. Social willingness to make trade-offs across timescales may vary over time as well. For example, when the financial crisis made short-term risks more pressing in 2008–2009, willingness to act on longer-term issues such as climate change declined.

---

14 Reeves, M., Levin, S.., and Fink, T., "Taming Complexity," *Harvard Business Review*, 2020.

A final challenge is that few effective mechanisms exist to govern collective action at the scale needed to take on sustainability threats. In particular, governance generally stops at country borders, whereas such problems are global in nature.

Solutions: Common goals, when articulated and agreed collectively, can act as a focusing mechanism to direct collective action – as seen in how John F. Kennedy's goal of putting a man on the moon within a decade became reality. As a more recent example, the Sustainable Development Goals set by the UN General Assembly established 17 sustainability objectives with specific targets for each, helping focus global efforts toward acting on those issues.

New data and analytical tools can help make progress toward those long-term goals more visible, increasing the ability to quantify trade-offs against short-term concerns. The rapid increase in ESG (environmental, social, and governance) data in business is one example of this phenomenon, and recent advances in big data and analytics promise to further increase transparency about sustainability risks and potential interventions.[15]

Finally, to overcome international governance challenges that inhibit top-down efforts, bottom-up solutions can advance progress. In some circumstances, polycentric approaches with multiple, overlapping coalitions of actors can tackle global challenges more effectively than top-down efforts.[16] For example, smaller groups of collaborators can change the incentives of participants by rewarding cooperators or penalizing non-participants, transforming a "prisoners' dilemma" (in which the only stable equilibrium is a lack of cooperation) into a "coordination game" (in which at least some degree of cooperation is possible).[17]

Common Insights on Multi-Timescale Strategy

When looking across these individual perspectives, several insights about the challenges and strategies involved in managing across multiple timescales begin to emerge. Though more work is required to operationalize solutions and specific prescriptions will vary by context, we can identify some initial principles that leaders can use as a basis for developing effective multi-timescale strategies.

---

15 Bril, Kell, and Rasche, *Sustainable Investing: A Path to a New Horizon*, Routledge, 2020.
16 Ostrom, E., Dietz, T., Dolsak, N., Stern P. C., Stonich, S., and Weber, E. U. (Eds.), *The Drama of the Commons*. Washington, D. C.: National Academies Press, 2002.
17 Chapin et al., "Earth Stewardship: Shaping a sustainable future through interacting policy and norm shifts," (forthcoming).

Embrace Contradiction

Leaders often seek a single correct answer that can be pursued consistently. But the nature of multi-timescale challenges is that the answers are often in fact contradictory – what is best in the short run may not be best in the long run. Leaders therefore need more sophisticated strategies that acknowledge contradiction. This might involve a strategy of switching between solutions at different points in time or in different parts of the business. And it might involve optimizing one timescale subject to a constraint set by another, such as maximizing the short term only subject to surviving in the long term.

Leverage simple rules for "good-enough" outcomes. When dealing with highly complex problems such as making trade-offs across intertwined timescales, it is tempting to try to analyze them in as much detail as possible and come up with an optimal solution. However, simple heuristics can often achieve satisfactory outcomes across a range of scenarios – and they may be more robust to uncertain and changing conditions than a precise optimization, even where it is feasible.[18] Leaders can identify and adopt heuristics that enable such "satisficing" strategies. An example of such a heuristic in business might be to avoid existential risk on any timescale – which does not necessarily produce the ideal trade-off between timescales but avoids making trade-offs that could result in the worst outcomes.

Design Decision Architectures that Promote a Balanced Focus

Individuals and organizations have inherent tendencies to focus on the most immediate issues. However, leaders can counter-balance this trend by designing decision-making architectures that promote a more balanced focus across timescales. Mechanisms for doing so include default-setting (have automatic decision rules that consider long-term needs as a default); division of responsibilities (ensuring some decision-makers are focused on longer timescales); and engineering incentives (metrics or rewards that encourage attention on longer timescales).

---

18 Simon, H., "Rational Choice and the Structure of the Environment," *Psychological Review*, 63 (2): 129–138, 1956.

Map and Understand the Larger System in Which You Operate

Businesses operate within larger economic, social, and environmental systems, which have feedback loops in both directions – businesses' actions affect the larger systems, and vice versa. Though predicting the exact behavior of such systems is rarely feasible, leaders can improve their understanding by explicitly mapping out the most impactful forces (accelerators or inhibitors of the system's workings) and understanding feedback loops and time constants, to identify more useful interventions. Because complex systems are often non-intuitive, conducting experiments at various levels of the system can help.

Use Adaptive Mechanisms

Trade-offs between timescales should not be considered a one-shot decision: as phenomena evolve over time, more will be learned about the viability of initial trade-offs, and the underlying situation may change. Therefore, leaders should implement structures or mechanisms that allow such decisions to be modulated over time. This allows the organization to tune the balance over time to avoid catastrophic outcomes on any one timescale.

Make Decisions with Progressive Commitment

To avoid the trap of premature "lock-in" – short-term decisions that constrain what can be done on longer timescales, potentially leading to loss of viability in the long run – leaders should aim to maintain reversibility in their decisions to the degree possible. A strategy for doing is to use progressive commitment: using change mechanisms that can be reversed at first (even if that comes at some cost) and graduating to more irreversible mechanisms only later when they are more certain to be needed in the long run.

One major insight emerging from our discussion is that long-term problems are generally collective problems. Many of the challenges on longer timescales that businesses face, such as maintaining sustainability of the environmental or economic context, cannot be sufficiently addressed only at the level of individual organizations. Instead, cooperation and collaboration are required (Figure 12.2).

This connects to a second set of solution principles involving collective action.

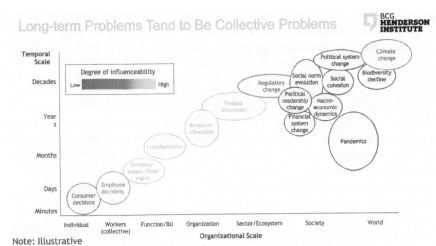

Note: Illustrative
Source: BCG Henderson Institute; inspired by Kavanaugh et al (2016), https://www.researchgate.
net/figure/Stommel-diagram-showing-time-and-space-scales-for-typical-biophysical-phenomenon
_fig3_305418677

Figure 12.2: Many of the challenges on longer timescales that businesses face cannot be
sufficiently addressed only at the level of individual organizations.

Don't Treat a "Prisoners' Dilemma" as Inevitable

Collective action problems can take the challenging form of a "prisoners' dilemma"
game. In such settings, the only stable equilibrium is one in which no actor cooper-
ates – because doing so would always be detrimental to their private interests –
even though full cooperation would be a better outcome for everybody. However, this state of affairs is not inevitable: in many situations, the payoffs can
be changed (through side payments or other mechanisms) to transform the game
into a "coordination" game, which has multiple stable equilibria, at least some of
which involve cooperation. This does not have to be done by an external authority. Decentralized action can also shift incentives, such as through the formation
of coalitions that promote and reward action toward the common good.

Create Better Metrics of Progress Toward Long-Term Goals

Reducing uncertainty about what and how much action is needed can shift incentives toward collective action. Businesses have developed a sophisticated
set of metrics for quantifying past performance, which may be a useful proxy
for the short-term outlook – but less progress has been made on metrics that

effectively quantify progress on long-term societal challenges. Leaders need to build on recent advances in analytics and ESG measurement to adopt new metrics that provide better transparency on such issues.

Leverage Financial Markets to Illuminate and Amplify Existing Beliefs

By providing a platform for a wide range of participants to make assessments about on future outcomes, financial markets can play a powerful role in bringing to light common beliefs about long-term issues. These price signals can guide collective resource allocation toward solving collective challenges. Though potentially powerful, markets only exist for a handful of primarily financial risks today, but the same mechanism could be applied to a wider range of phenomena – including climate change.

Articulate Compelling Goals and Narratives

Articulating a vision of the future can help make it a reality. Compelling goals or narratives can act as a focusing mechanism by coordinating beliefs around what other actors should strive to achieve, and they can make long-term issues more salient. Leaders can harness this power to build momentum for effective long-term action within their own organizations, such as by articulating a positive purpose that their business serves. They can also support the development of broader goals and narratives that focus collective action against broader social problems.

Pursue Bottom-Up Approaches

Top-down authority is not the only way to bring about effective change on large-scale problems. Bottom-up collaboration is also capable of making sufficient progress and has advantages in terms of innovation and stability (especially in a polycentric framework). While leaders should encourage and promote effective regulation, they can also promote bottom-up action, such as collaborating within or across industries, to create momentum on common challenges.

As the tension between economic growth and planetary and societal sustainability becomes more acute, the challenge of managing on multiple timescales will become more important. In order to meet that challenge, leaders in business and society will have to build and adopt a new toolkit. Though there is more work to be done on defining what that entails, we hope the insights outlined here can form a starting point.

Martin Reeves, Kevin Whitaker, and Saumeet Nanda

Chapter 13
Fractal Strategy: Responding to COVID-19 Effectively on Multiple Timescales

As the COVID-19 outbreak spread across the globe, organizations were initially focused on *reacting* to the immediate issues posed by the epidemic. However, as the crisis unfolded, several other challenges rapidly emerged: preparing for a potential recession in the near term; anticipating an eventual rebound in demand (initially when social distancing restrictions are relaxed, and later when consumer and business confidence returns); and ultimately *reimagining* operations, products, and business models for the post-crisis world.

Crucially, even in the early stages of the outbreak, leaders could wait to take on these challenges sequentially – they already had to begin considering and acting on the longer-term implications of the crisis, due to the lead times required to build and execute, and the speed and unpredictability with which events can unfold. During critical periods in history, pivotal changes have often been concentrated in a very short period of time, and the "new normal" can arrive very rapidly. We also have the agency to shape history provided we act preemptively. In the case of COVID-19, as consumers adjusted to life under social distancing restrictions, they formed new habits that may persist long after the outbreak, and businesses' actions during the crisis shaped the formation of those behaviors.

In other words, leaders and organizations need to consider all levels of strategic response – reaction, recession, rebound, and re-imagination – simultaneously. Yet our benchmarking shows that many companies delayed responding to the longer-term implications to focus first on more immediate issues.

This is an example of a more general challenge that business leaders increasingly face: the need to think and operate on multiple timescales simultaneously. Companies need to manage longer timescales to avoid potential disruption from social, technological, or economic shifts. (See Chapter 11, "The Challenge of Slow.") And they need to manage shorter timescales to perform well in the current business to maintain viability and fund long term opportunities, especially as competitive advantage becomes less persistent.[1]

---

1 https://sloanreview.mit.edu/article/fighting-the-gravity-of-average-performance/.

https://doi.org/10.1515/9783110755381-013

This challenge has increased in a world where business-relevant time-scales have been stretched in both directions – from the speed of algorithms (operating on milliseconds) to the increased importance of planetary and social timescales (operating over decades). And critical timescales are now converging: issues that could previously be considered far off in the future, such as climate change, have reached a point where they directly affect and require action from business today. As the response to COVID-19 shows, companies' traditional methods for managing multiple timescales are often not up to this challenge.

Companies Primarily Focused on Near-Term Responses

To better understand how businesses have structured their response to the COVID-19 crisis, we conducted a survey of more than 300 companies across 55 countries and 24 industries in March and April of 2020. Not surprisingly, we found that nearly all companies had reacted to the immediate threats: About 85% of companies had taken multiple measures to protect the health and safety of employees and ensure business continuity.

Roughly 60% of companies had taken measures to plan for and navigate a likely recession, such as putting cost control measures in place and revising capital investment plans. In contrast, only about 40% of companies had taken measures to prepare for a potential rebound of demand, and very few had begun reimagining the business for a post-COVID-19 world.

And while the distinct challenges of reaction, recession, rebound, and reimagination will likely affect all businesses, only about 10% of survey respondents had started planning on all four pillars simultaneously (Figure 13.1).

Traditional Mechanisms for Managing Multiple Time Scales Fall Short

Companies do have a few traditional ways for balancing multiple timescales. However, the extreme challenges posed by COVID-19 have exposed their limitations.

One method is applying a discount rate to expected cashflows and computing a net present value for various options in order to make choices across different

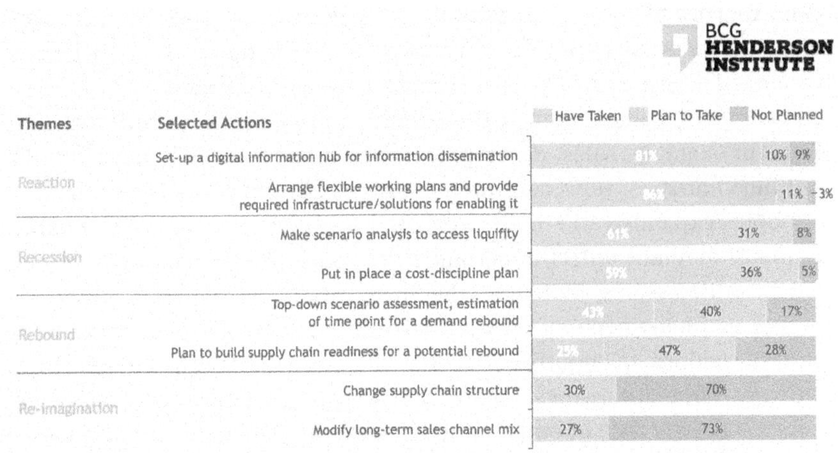

BCG
HENDERSON
INSTITUTE

Themes	Selected Actions	Have Taken	Plan to Take	Not Planned
Reaction	Set-up a digital information hub for information dissemination	81%	10%	9%
	Arrange flexible working plans and provide required infrastructure/solutions for enabling it	86%	11%	3%
Recession	Make scenario analysis to access liquifity	61%	31%	8%
	Put in place a cost-discipline plan	59%	36%	5%
Rebound	Top-down scenario assessment, estimation of time point for a demand rebound	43%	40%	17%
	Plan to build supply chain readiness for a potential rebound	25%	47%	28%
Re-imagination	Change supply chain structure	30%		70%
	Modify long-term sales channel mix	27%		73%

Source: BCG COVID-19 Company Survey through 15 April; BCG Henderson Institute Analysis

Figure 13.1: How businesses have structured their response to the COVID-19 crisis.

timescales. But many opportunities cannot be easily quantified in this way. For instance, potential long-term shifts in customer behaviors that result from COVID-19 can be hard to calibrate and there are multiple plausible scenarios. Human decision-makers are also known to apply hyperbolic discounting (applying a different discount rate at different times), which can distort time trade-offs. This can become more pronounced in the heat of a crisis, when the focus shifts to the short term. Finally, discounting is complicated by path dependence, in which actions taken today will shape which opportunities are available tomorrow.

Organizational hierarchy is another implicit mechanism for managing multiple timescales: employees at operational levels focus on day-to-day issues while senior leaders focus on longer-term strategic decisions. However, if a short-term issue arises that requires immediate structural action, hierarchical organizations can lack reliable override mechanisms to reallocate issues between levels. And when senior leaders are spurred to act against immediate threats, the balance can then shift away from longer-term opportunities, as demonstrated by many organizations' responses to COVID-19. Furthermore, there are time lags in transmitting and translating information up and down the hierarchy.

Some organizations have *mixed planning cycles* on different, fixed timescales, such as a detailed annual operating plan and a three- or five-year strategic plan. However, pre-determined timescales may not be appropriate for each specific situation. For instance, construction projects typically operate on extended planning cycles, but Chinese construction firm CSCEC adopted a

24-hour cadence to construct two hospitals for coronavirus patients in ten days. Strategy processes need to be modulated according to the drumbeat set by the environment, rather than be fixed according to internal precedent.

Finally, companies often have *separate units* focused on different timescales. For example, sales, development, and research usually have very different time horizons. However, the timescales of business are becoming more continuous, expanded and intertwined, and a fixed number of pre-determined timeframes may not reflect important shifts, such as the emergence of new, algorithmic timescales. Moreover, the "long term" and the "short term" can converge as phenomena speed up. For example, new medical products are usually developed on multi-year cycles, but the COVID-19 crisis demanded greatly accelerated timelines. Finally, the relevant timeframe may not be predictable (as in the case of potential new waves of infections) and thus cannot be boxed into any fixed timescale.

Strategy on Multiple Timescales

A fundamental challenge in realizing a multi-timescale strategy is that different timescales call for different strategic approaches. We have previously identified five distinct approaches to strategy and execution which reflect the predictability, malleability, and harshness of the business environment to which they are applied (see Chapter 8, "Your Strategy Process Needs a Strategy"):

1. *Classical strategy:* For markets that are predictable, analyze the drivers, plan your actions, and execute against stable plans.
2. *Adaptive strategy:* For markets that are unpredictable, vary your bets, select the most promising ones, and scale them up quickly to capitalize on shifting opportunities.
3. *Visionary strategy:* For markets that can be predicted and shaped, envision the future, build a business to pursue the defined vision, and persist in pursuing that goal.
4. *Shaping strategy:* For markets that can be shaped but not predicted, engage a broad ecosystem of partners, orchestrate their actions, and co-evolve together.
5. *Renewal strategy:* For harsh markets and situations (such as a crisis or recession), react promptly and pragmatically to avoid danger, economize on resources, and later pivot to growth.

The COVID-19 crisis illustrates how issues on different timescales often require the application of different strategic approaches. For many large companies, day-to-day operations and demand have tended to be highly predictable, so a classical strategy based on planning and disciplined execution often dominates. However, during the COVID-19 crisis, markets became unpredictable even on short time-scales, requiring an adaptive approach, focused on rapid learning and real-time adjustment. For example, as the outbreak began in Italy, energy infrastructure operator SNAM recognized the risk to its dispatching center, which manages gas distribution.[2] It adapted rapidly, purchasing residential facilities, testing all dispatching center staff, and identifying a group of healthy employees to work and live on the premises. This response ensured that dispatching center staff were protected from the outbreak even as it intensified in surrounding area, and operational viability was maintained.

Over timescales of a few months, the effects of government-imposed lock-downs and a recession threatened many businesses' survival, forcing them to operate a renewal strategy. And while there is high uncertainty about the post-crisis future, consumer preferences will likely be malleable as they adjust to the forced changes in their lifestyles, calling for a visionary or shaping strategy.

The crisis also illustrates how business relevant timescales can rapidly change or converge. For example, pymetrics, a neuroscience/AI-based hiring and talent deployment start-up, initially developed a product roadmap for the year that prior-itized its hiring support offering. However, many companies reduced hiring plans as the outbreak unfolded and instead focused on redeploying their existing work-force. As a result, pymetrics shifted to focus on redeployment offerings, which had previously been considered a longer-term priority.[3] The company worked together with partners to build and orchestrate a platform for matching furloughed workers to job opportunities.

As new timescales emerge and existing timescales converge, businesses need to cultivate *temporal ambidexterity* – the ability to apply different strategic approaches to different problems on different timescales, and to modulate the approach according to changing circumstances.

---

2 https://bcghendersoninstitute.com/lessons-from-the-covid-crisis-marco-alver%C3%A0-ceo-of-snam-3a5287063353.

3 https://bcghendersoninstitute.com/leading-through-the-covid-crisis-frida-polli-ceo-of-pymetrics-5c361a742550.

Realizing Fractal Strategy

Understand the Required Clock Speed and Strategic Approach of Each Business

Within any company, each business line or geographic unit may have different relevant timescales and require correspondingly different approaches to strategy. Hence, leaders need to identify and apply the right strategic approaches in the right place at the right time. For example, consumer packaged goods companies are generally used to operating in a classical environment with predictable demand. But some business lines, such as health and safety products, faced temporary spikes in short-term demand, requiring an adaptive approach. Other business units may have been more stable in the short run but were exposed to long-term changes in distribution models as consumer activity shifted online, perhaps requiring a shaping strategy to collaborate on new channels and partnerships.

Master the Capabilities Underpinning Different Approaches to Strategy

Leaders in established companies are often used to working in classical (stable, predictable) environments, but a classical approach is not always optimal. In order to address challenges on all timescales, a company must be able to apply the entire palette of strategic approaches. Traditional top-down strategy is not feasible on algorithmic timescales; companies must instead take an adaptive approach, integrating AI, data platforms, and decision systems in autonomous learning loops. For example, global food giant Danone S.A. dealt with supply chain uncertainties by feeding AI tools with new data on COVID-19 spread patterns to help distribute materials and keep their factories running. And for slow-moving issues, classical strategy will miss opportunities to envision and shape the market for advantage, such as harnessing the power of organizational imagination.

Master the Ability to Act on Multiple Timescales Simultaneously

Balancing short-term exploitation and long-term exploration is a perennial business challenge, made more critical by the emergence and convergence of new timescales. Businesses face many short-term challenges that naturally demand leaders' attention. However, our research shows companies that act preemptively in the face of disruptions outperform those who wait longer, reinforcing the need to attend to longer-term issues early.[4] For instance, in response to the COVID-19 crisis, LEGO set up a small team to think about the post-crisis future even while most of management was still focused on steering through the immediate crisis.[5]

As the business environment becomes more complex and diverse, traditional approaches to strategy will be increasingly limiting. Businesses can use crises like COVID-19 as an opportunity to revisit and strengthen their approaches to strategy. By being able to vary the clock speed of each part of the business and think on multiple timescales simultaneously, leaders can improve their odds of succeeding in this crisis and the next one.

Coda: Inspiration from Biology

Companies need to operate on multiple timescales to respond to the biological threat posed by the novel coronavirus. But they can also turn to biology for inspiration. Biological systems have evolved to survive both short- and long-run challenges, and their behaviors illustrate some key principles of a multi-timescale strategy (Figure 13.2).

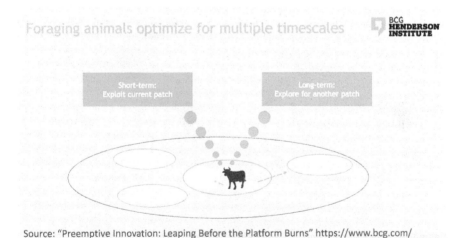

Source: "Preemptive Innovation: Leaping Before the Platform Burns" https://www.bcg.com/publications/2018/leaping-before-platform-burns-increasing-necessity-preemptive-innovation

Figure 13.2: Biological systems illustrate some key principles of a multi-timescale strategy.

---

4 https://www.bcg.com/publications/2018/preemptive-transformation-fix-it-before-it-breaks.
5 https://bcghendersoninstitute.com/lessons-from-the-covid-crisis-j%C3%B8rgen-vig-knudstorp-chairman-of-lego-brand-group-ab10ea135c60.

Optimizing for multiple timescales: Animals that forage in patchy environments face a trade-off between feeding from their current patch (which provides short-term benefit but eventually exhausts that patch) and searching for a new patch (which incurs immediate costs but offers greater long term security). Many animals therefore begin searching for a new patch at the optimal point to balance short- and long-term benefits – an example of what is known as the Marginal Value Theorem.[6] When is the right time for your business to start looking for a new patch?

Matching response mechanisms to timescales: Organisms respond to a change in the environment by making adjustments that cascade from short-term to long-term with decreasing reversibility, using different mechanisms (Figure 13.3).[7] For example, if the environment becomes colder, animals might immediately shiver, which is fast and easily reversible. But if cooling persists, they will make more substantial adjustments, such as sheltering, moving to warmer places, or increasing fat storage, which are moderately reversible. If changes persist, they may eventually evolve genetically to become better adapted to cold environments. What are the cascading adaptation mechanisms for your business?

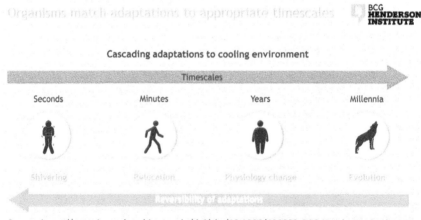

Source: https://www.journals.uchicago.edu/doi/abs/10.1086/408082; BCG Henderson Institure

Figure 13.3: Organisms respond to a change in the environment by making adjustments that cascade from short-term to long-term with decreasing reversibility, using different mechanisms.

---

6 https://www.sciencedaily.com/releases/2011/06/110606152210.htm.
7 https://pubmed.ncbi.nlm.nih.gov/4411986/.

Applying different types of strategies for different environments: Reproductive strategies can be divided two categories: r-selection, which involves producing many highly diverse offspring with low selection pressure and parental investment; and K-selection, which involves fewer offspring with higher parental investment.[8] Species such as bacteria and rodents that operate in disrupted or uncertain environments tend to use r-selection strategies to ensure many "shots on goal," whereas species such as elephants or humans that operate in more stable environments tend to use K-selection strategies (Figure 13.4). Which innovation or new business build strategy should your business adopt in the current environment?

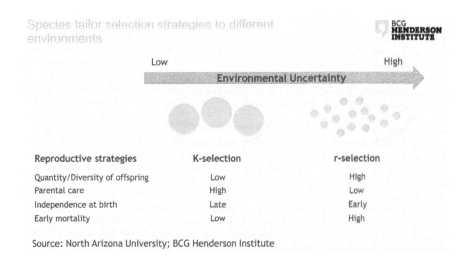

Species tailor selection strategies to different environments

BCG HENDERSON INSTITUTE

Low   High

Environmental Uncertainty

Reproductive strategies	K-selection	r-selection
Quantity/Diversity of offspring	Low	High
Parental care	High	Low
Independence at birth	Late	Early
Early mortality	Low	High

Source: North Arizona University; BCG Henderson Institute

Figure 13.4: Reproductive strategies can be divided two categories: K-selection, which involves producing fewer offspring with higher parental investment; and r-selection, which involves more offspring with lower parental investment.

---

8 https://www.jstor.org/stable/2459020?seq=1#metadata_info_tab_contents.

List of Figures

1.1   Three- and two-generalist configurations appear to have the greatest stability and to act as the strongest "basins of attraction" —— 4

1.2   The evolution of the U.S. rental car industry illustrates the rule of three and four —— 5

2.1   The relationship between experience in *fulfilling* demand and experience in *shaping* demand —— 10

2.2   Facebook shaped demand for its services faster than rival MySpace —— 12

3.1   Companies using time-based competition could produce fewer goods but with greater diversity and quality than their competitors at lower cost —— 15

3.2   U.S. households by type of phone ownership 1900–2011 —— 17

4.1   Market share is no longer a direct predictor of sustained performance —— 21

4.2   The breakdown of the relationship between relative market share and sustained competitiveness —— 23

5.1   Essential attributes for survival in a changing business environment —— 30

5.2   The four styles of adaptive strategy —— 31

7.1   Many markets are ripe for shaping strategies —— 41

8.1   Five broad approaches to strategy —— 46

8.2   Variations in strategy processes —— 51

8.3   Metaprocesses within strategy processes —— 52

9.1   The sets of traits needed to set and execute strategy effectively —— 61

9.2   The five strategic environments and traits for success —— 62

9.3   All approaches can be learned, but at different rates —— 63

10.1   The five new imperatives of competition —— 72

10.2   Netflix's algorithms take in behavioral data from the company's video streaming platform and automatically provide dynamic, personalized recommendations for each user —— 73

10.3   Today's most valuable and fastest-growing businesses are disproportionately young technology companies —— 75

10.4   Older and larger companies have less vitality – the capacity for sustainable growth and reinvention —— 77

10.5   Uncertainty is high on many fronts —— 79

11.1   The age distribution of the world population is moving from a pyramid shape to a rectangle —— 82

11.2   Economists forecast steady decline in world GDP growth —— 83

11.3   The Japanese labor force and consumption have been more or less stagnant for the past 20 years —— 84

11.4   Hierarchical organizational structures largely remain pyramid shaped, creating a shortage of young workers for entry-level jobs and a surplus of older workers —— 86

12.1   In evolution, organisms often adopt a strategy of progressive irreversibility —— 98

12.2   Many of the challenges on longer timescales that businesses face cannot be sufficiently addressed only at the level of individual organizations —— 107

13.1   How businesses have structured their response to the COVID-19 crisis —— 111

https://doi.org/10.1515/9783110755381-014

13.2 Biological systems illustrate some key principles of a multi-timescale strategy —— **115**

13.3 Organisms respond to a change in the environment by making adjustments that cascade from short-term to long-term with decreasing reversibility, using different mechanisms —— **116**

13.4 Reproductive strategies can be divided two categories: K-selection, which involves producing fewer offspring with higher parental investment; and r-selection, which involves more offspring with lower parental investment —— **117**

Index

23andMe 49

adaptive advantage XII
AEON 86
Agco 5
AIG 96
Alibaba 17
Amazon 65
ambidexterity 11
American Express 50
Anne Maria Eikeset 96
Anne Wojcicki 49
Apple 15
Arabesque 96
ARM Holdings 11
AT&T 5
Avis 5

Big Five 62
bounded rationality 99
Bruce Henderson XII

chemical pollution 103
choice architectures 99
Clay Christensen 35
climate change 103
CNH 5
Coasean logic 74
comparative advantage 99
COVID-19 109
CSCEC 111

Danone S.A. 114
David Young 96
degree of exploration 31
degree of intentionality 31
degree of modification 31
degree of proactivity 31
disaster preparedness 103
diversity 51
dynamism 52

ecosystems 79
Eddie Cue 66

Electrolux 5
Elke Weber 96
Enterprise Holdings 5
Equifax 5
ESG 104
Experian 5

Facebook 12

GE 5
General Electric 47
General Martin Dempsey 36
Georg Kell 96
George Stalk 15
gig economy 74
Google 23

Haier 18, 53
Hertz 5
Hitachi 85
hyperbolic discounting 87

Imagination 38, 46
Indian School of Business 57
Indra Nooyi 52
ING Bank Netherlands 53
integrated learning architectures 73
IoT 76

Jack Ma 54
Jeff Immelt 47
Jeremy Stoppelman 16
John Bunch 65
John Deere 5, 76
John F. Kennedy 104
John Stone 76
Jony Ive 49

Keiichiro Takahara 89
Ken Chenault 50

Lars Rebien Sørensen 40
LEGO 115
Line 86

https://doi.org/10.1515/9783110755381-015

Linux 65
Lyft 74

Mahindra 54
Marginal Value Theorem 116
Maria Hancock 96
Mars 48
Max Weber 35
McDonald's 32
metaprocesses 51
Microsoft 64
Ming Zeng 54, 67
Mitchell Modell 16
Modell's Sporting Goods 16

Netflix 12
Nick Silitch 96
Nike 18
Nitori 86
Norges Bank 96
Novo Nordisk 39

organizational inertia 88

Paul Michaels 48
PepsiCo 52
Peter Hancock 96
Peter Turchin 96
Philipp Carlsson-Szlezak 96
polarization 78
price signals 100
prisoners' dilemma 94
Procter & Gamble 85
Prudential Financial 96
pymetrics 57

Qualcomm 12

Rational Experiential Inventory 62
Red Hat 49
resilience 29, 79
Ryutaro Hashimoto 84

Satya Nadella 64
SB Technology 86

"shaping" strategies XII
Simon Levin 96
Sir Hiram Maxim 39
slow-moving forces XII
SNAM 113
Southwest Airlines 39
species depletion 103
Stephanie Forrest 96
Steve Jobs 66
strategy 45
strategy games 58

TejPavan Gandhok 57
the experience curve XII
The Experimenter 32
the growth-share matrix XII
The Migrator 32
the ostrich effect 88
the rule of three and four XII
The Sprinter 32
The Voyager 32
Thomas Edison 39
Tim Cook 15, 66
time-based competition XII
T-Mobile 5
Tom Hout 15
Transunion 5

Uber 74
Unicharm 84
UPS 17

Vanguard Car Rental 5
Virgin 32
vitality 91

Waymo 76
Whirlpool 5
Whole Foods 76

Yelp 16

Zappos 65
Zara 32